Reading and Writing to Learn

Reading and Writing to Learn

Strategies across the Curriculum

Katherine Wiesolek Kuta

Teacher Ideas Press

An imprint of Libraries Unlimited
Westport, Connecticut • London

Library of Congress Cataloging-in-Publication Data

Kuta, Katherine Wiesolek, 1952-
    Reading and writing to learn : strategies across the curriculum / Katherine Kuta.
        p. cm.
    Includes bibliographical references.
    ISBN 978-1-59158-585-5 (alk. paper)
    1. Language arts—Correlation with content subjects. 2. Lesson planning. I. Title.
    LB1575.8.K87   2008
    372.6—dc22   2007048820

British Library Cataloguing in Publication Data is available.

Library of Congress Catalog Card Number: 2007048820
ISBN: 978-1-59158-585-6

First published in 2008

Libraries Unlimited/Teacher Ideas Press, 88 Post Road West, Westport, CT 06881
A Member of the Greenwood Publishing Group, Inc.
www.lu.com

Printed in the United States of America

The paper used in this book complies with the
Permanent Paper Standard issued by the National
Information Standards Organization (Z39.48–1984).

10   9   8   7   6   5   4   3   2   1

This book is dedicated to special people who have been connected to me in my life.

My daughter, Melanie, who is now 15, who talks about reading and writing with me and truly has been an inspiration for me to write.

My nieces and nephews, Kristine, Joe, Karly, Laura, Elizabeth, Richard, Katie, Jarrett, John, and Hannah, who know that their aunt always talks about books with them and promotes the importance of education for success.

My students at Maine East High School in Illinois, who have grown as readers and writers, and have matured into lifelong learners.

Contents

List of Handouts. xv
Preface. xvii
Introduction. xix

Part 1
Reading to Learn

Activity 1: Reading to Learn (Pre- or Post-): Content Continuum. 3
    Purpose of the Activity 3
    How to Use the Activity 3
    Evaluation 4
    Variation(s) 4

Activity 2: Previewing: Text Chapter, Magazine, and Newspaper. 9
    Purpose of the Activity 9
    How to Use the Activity 9
    Evaluation 10
    Variation(s) 10

Activity 3: Previewing, Scanning, and Skimming. 15
    Purpose of the Activity 15
    How to Use the Activity 15
    Evaluation 16
    Variation(s) 16

Activity 4: Asking Questions to Find the Main Idea and Details 22
    Purpose of the Activity 22
    How to Use the Activity 22
    Evaluation 22
    Variation(s) 23

Activity 5: Vocabulary Mapping 27
    Purpose of the Activity 27
    How to Use the Activity 27
    Evaluation 27
    Variation(s) 27

Activity 6: Visualizing Yourself Using Reading and Writing in 10 to 15 Years. 29
    Purpose of the Activity 29
    How to Use the Activity 29
    Evaluation 30
    Variation(s) 30

Activity 7: Visualizing: Drawing to Remember 32
    Purpose of the Activity 32
    How to Use the Activity 32
    Evaluation 33
    Variation(s) 33

Activity 8: Symbolism on the Penny and the Dollar Bill 35
  Purpose of the Activity 35
  How to Use the Activity 35
  Evaluation 36
  Variation(s) 36

Activity 9: Inference: Hidden Meaning in Advertisements 44
  Purpose of the Activity 44
  How to Use the Activity 44
  Evaluation 44
  Variation(s) 44

Activity 10: Inference Practice with Literacy Quotations 47
  Purpose of the Activity 47
  How to Use the Activity 47
  Evaluation 47
  Variation(s) 47

Activity 11: Making Inferences with Cartoons 55
  Purpose of the Activity 55
  How to Use the Activity 55
  Evaluation 56
  Variation(s) 56

Activity 12: Predicting and Making Inferences with Photos/Pictures 59
  Purpose of the Activity 59
  How to Use the Activity 59
  Evaluation 59
  Variation(s) 59

Activity 13: Inferences: Visualizing and Illustrating Significant Quotes 63
  Purpose of the Activity 63
  How to Use the Activity 63
  Evaluation 63
  Variation(s) 63

Activity 14: Making Inferences Using Visuals 65
  Purpose of the Activity 65
  How to Use the Activity 65
  Evaluation 65
  Variation(s) 66

Activity 15: Monitoring One's Own Comprehension 76
  Purpose of the Activity 76
  How to Use the Activity 76
  Evaluation 76
  Variation(s) 76

Activity 16: Connecting to Text: Cooperative PowerPoint Review 78
  Purpose of the Activity 78
  How to Use the Activity 78
  Evaluation 79
  Variation(s) 79

Activity 17: Using Metaphor to Increase Comprehension 82
    Purpose of the Activity 82
    How to Use the Activity 82
    Evaluation 82
    Variation(s) 82

**Activity 18: Creating Metaphors for the Deeper Meaning Structures of Comprehension,
or "What Good Readers Do!"** 84
    Purpose of the Activity 84
    How to Use the Activity 84
    Evaluation 84
    Variation(s) 85

Activity 19: Fluency: Rapid Retrieval Strategy 90
    Purpose of the Activity 90
    How to Use the Activity 90
    Evaluation 90
    Variation(s) 90

Activity 20: Practicing Fluency with Children's Books 93
    Purpose of the Activity 93
    How to Use the Activity 93
    Evaluation 94
    Variation(s) 94

Part 2
Reading and Writing to Learn, Involving
Affective and Cooperative Learning

Activity 21: Cooperative Learning: Appointment Clock 99
    Purpose of the Activity 99
    How to Use the Activity 99
    Evaluation 99
    Variation(s) 99

Activity 22: Affective Learning: Tombstone Test 101
    Purpose of the Activity 101
    How to Use the Activity 101
    Evaluation 101
    Variation(s) 101

Activity 23: People Search: Preview or Review 103
    Purpose of the Activity 103
    How to Use the Activity 103
    Evaluation 104
    Variation(s) 104

Activity 24: Share an Idea and Get an Idea 110
    Purpose of the Activity 110
    How to Use the Activity 110
    Evaluation 111
    Variation(s) 111

Activity 25: Affective Reading and Writing Survey 115
   Purpose of the Activity 115
   How to Use the Activity 115
   Evaluation 115
   Variation(s) 115

Activity 26: Parent–Child Questionnaire 117
   Purpose of the Activity 117
   How to Use the Activity 117
   Evaluation 117
   Variation(s) 117

Activity 27: Writing: "Positive Feel Good" Messages 120
   Purpose of the Activity 120
   How to Use the Activity 120
   Evaluation 120
   Variation(s) 121

Activity 28: Cooperative Learning Using Jigsaw and Notetaking 123
   Purpose of the Activity 123
   How to Use the Activity 123
   Evaluation 124
   Variation(s) 124

Activity 29: Cooperative Learning: Information Poster 127
   Purpose of the Activity 127
   How to Use the Activity 127
   Evaluation 128
   Variation(s) 128

Activity 30: Reading Critically for Understanding 130
   Purpose of the Activity 130
   How to Use the Activity 130
   Evaluation 130
   Variation(s) 130

Activity 31: Connecting to Poetry 132
   Purpose of the Activity 132
   How to Use the Activity 132
   Evaluation 132
   Variation(s) 132

Activity 32: Understanding Nonfiction Using a Magazine 134
   Purpose of the Activity 134
   How to Use the Activity 134
   Evaluation 135
   Variation(s) 135

Activity 33: Bookmark of Information 138
   Purpose of the Activity 138
   How to Use the Activity 138
   Evaluation 138
   Variation(s) 138

Activity 34: Using *Newsweek* Magazine for Reading and Writing 140
   Purpose of the Activity 140
   How to Use the Activity 140
   Evaluation 140
   Variation(s) 141

Activity 35: Reading and Writing: Comprehending *Reader's Digest* Magazine 143
   Purpose of the Activity 143
   How to Use the Activity 143
   Evaluation 143
   Variation(s) 143

Activity 36: Literacy Circle: Reading for Information 147
   Purpose of the Activity 147
   How to Use the Activity 147
   Evaluation 147
   Variation(s) 147

Activity 37: What I Learned While Reading 149
   Purpose of the Activity 149
   How to Use the Activity 149
   Evaluation 149
   Variation(s) 149

Activity 38: Writing a Story Based on a Picture/Photograph 151
   Purpose of the Activity 151
   How to Use the Activity 151
   Evaluation 152
   Variation(s) 152

Activity 39: Using Music and Dance to Learn 155
   Purpose of the Activity 155
   How to Use the Activity 155
   Evaluation 155
   Variation(s) 155

Activity 40: Information Poster 158
   Purpose of the Activity 158
   How to Use the Activity 158
   Evaluation 158
   Variation(s) 158

Part 3
Writing to Learn

Activity 41: Writing to Learn: Two-Column Notetaking 163
   Purpose of the Activity 163
   How to Use the Activity 163
   Evaluation 163
   Variation(s) 164

Activity 42: Writing to Learn: Foldable 167
   Purpose of the Activity 167
   How to Use the Activity 167
   Evaluation 167
   Variation(s) 167

Activity 43: Writing to Learn: Processing Information Boxes 172
   Purpose of the Activity 172
   How to Use the Activity 172
   Evaluation 172
   Variation(s) 173

Activity 44: Writing: Daily Reflections 175
   Purpose of the Activity 175
   How to Use the Activity 175
   Evaluation 175
   Variation(s) 175

Activity 45: Writing Poetry: Metonymy 177
   Purpose of the Activity 177
   How to Use the Activity 177
   Evaluation 177
   Variation(s) 177

Activity 46: Writing: The Power of Three 179
   Purpose of the Activity 179
   How to Use the Activity 179
   Evaluation 179
   Variation(s) 179

Activity 47: Writing: Facts vs. Opinions 182
   Purpose of the Activity 182
   How to Use the Activity 182
   Evaluation 182
   Variation(s) 182

Activity 48: Writing a Memo 184
   Purpose of the Activity 184
   How to Use the Activity 184
   Evaluation 184
   Variation(s) 184

Activity 49: Writing an E-mail for a Specific Audience 186
   Purpose of the Activity 186
   How to Use the Activity 186
   Evaluation 186
   Variation(s) 186

Activity 50: Writing a Want Ad 188
   Purpose of the Activity 188
   How to Use the Activity 188
   Evaluation 188
   Variation(s) 188

Activity 51: Writing: Say It with Pictures 192
   Purpose of the Activity 192
   How to Use the Activity 192
   Evaluation 192
   Variation(s) 192

Activity 52: Writing a Friendly Letter to a Pen Pal 195
   Purpose of the Activity 195
   How to Use the Activity 195
   Evaluation 195
   Variation(s) 196

Activity 53: Letter to Next Year's Students: How to Be Successful in Class! 198
   Purpose of the Activity 198
   How to Use the Activity 198
   Evaluation 198
   Variation(s) 198

Activity 54: Steps in the Writing Process 200
   Purpose of the Activity 200
   How to Use the Activity 200
   Evaluation 200
   Variation(s) 200

Activity 55: Formal Writing Plan for Argumentation (Persuasive Writing) 202
   Purpose of the Activity 202
   How to Use the Activity 202
   Evaluation 202
   Variation(s) 203

Activity 56: Timed Writing Checklist 208
   Purpose of the Activity 208
   How to Use the Activity 208
   Evaluation 208
   Variation(s) 208

Activity 57: Writing to Learn: Writing for a Younger Audience 210
   Purpose of the Activity 210
   How to Use the Activity 210
   Evaluation 211
   Variation(s) 211

Activity 58: Writing: Paraphrasing 213
   Purpose of the Activity 213
   How to Use the Activity 213
   Evaluation 213
   Variation(s) 213

Activity 59: Summary Writing 215
   Purpose of the Activity 215
   How to Use the Activity 215
   Evaluation 216
   Variation(s) 216

Activity 60: Letter of Self-Evaluation to the Teacher 218
   Purpose of the Activity 218
   How to Use the Activity 218
   Evaluation 218
   Variation(s) 218

   References 221

List of Handouts

Part 1: Reading to Learn

1A–1D. Reading to Learn: Content Curriculum 5–8
2A. Previewing a Textbook Reading 11
2B. Previewing Magazines and Reading to Learn 12
2C. Previewing a Newspaper: Scavenger Hunt 13
3A. Scanning and Skimming a Chapter 17
3B. Skimming a Chapter 18
3C. Scanning and Skimming on the Internet 20
4A. Asking Questions about the Text 24
4B. Questions: Explicit vs. Implicit 25
4C. Main Ideas: Informational Page to Share 26
5. Vocabulary Mapping 28
6. Visualizing: Using Reading and Writing in 10–15 Years 31
7. Visualizing: Drawing to Remember 34
8A. Visualization ad Observation of a Penny 37
8B. Visualization: Designing a Coin 39
8C. Making Observations and Understanding Symbolism Using a Dollar Bill. 41
8D. Creating Your Own Dollar Bill 43
9. Inferencing: Finding the Hidden Messages in Advertisements 45
10A. Inference Practice with Literary Quotations 48
10B. Discussion Sheet: Inferencing 49
10C. Making Inferences Using Famous Quotes 52
11. Making Inferences with Cartoons 57
12. Predicting and Inferring with Photos 61
13. Inferences: Significant Quotes 64
14A. Making Inferences Based on Objects 67
14B. Using Visuals on Hobbies to Practice Inference 69
14C. Inferences Drawn from Clipart 70
14D. Inferences Based on Signs 72
14E. Using Clipart to Make Inferences about Yourself 74
14F. Making Inferences Based on Classmates' Objects 75
15. Monitoring Comprehension 77
16. Connecting to Text for Increased Comprehension. 80
17. Writing to Learn: Using Metaphor. 83
18A. Synthesizing: Creating Metaphors for Comprehension 86
18B. Synthesis of Content 87
18C. Synthesizing Content Notes 88
18D. Using Comprehension Strategies to Reflect on Words. 89
19A. Reference Journal Summary 91
19B. Rapid Retrieval of Information for Increasing Fluency and Comprehension 92
20A. Reading to Learn: Practicing Fluency with Children's Books 95
20B. Using Children's Books for Critical Thinking 96

Part 2: Reading and Writing to Learn, Involving Affective and Cooperative Learning

21. Cooperative Learning: Appointment Clock...................................... 100
22. Affective Learning: Tombstone Test.. 102

Part 2: Reading and Writing to Learn, Involving Affective and Cooperative Learning(*Cont.*)
23A. Student People Search: "Get to Know Your Classmates" 105
23B. Student Content People Search 107
23C. Generalization vs. Detail 109
24A. Cooperative and Affective Learning: Share an Idea and Get an Idea 112
24B. Cooperative and Affective Learning: Share an Idea and Get an Idea Using Notes 113
24C. Record of Ideas from Student Sharing 114
25. Affective Reading and Writing Survey 116
26. Parent–Child Questionnaire 118
27. Writing: Positive Messages 122
28A. Jigsaw Note Sheet 125
28B. Cooperative Learning: Sharing Information 126
29. Cooperative Learning: Information Poster 129
30. Reading Critically 131
31. Finding a Poem to Connect to Self, Text in Class, or the World 133
32. Understanding a Magazine Article 136
33. Creating an Informational Bookmark 139
34. Reading and Writing Using *Newsweek* 142
35. Reading and Writing Using *Reader's Digest* 144
36. Reading for Information 148
37. What I Learned by Reading _____ 150
38. Using a Visual to Create and Write a Story 153
39. Using Music and Dance to Learn 156
40. Promotional Ad Poster 159

Part 3: Writing to Learn
41A. Two-Column System of Notetaking 165
41B. Notetaking to Learn and Remember 166
42A. Writing to Learn: Notetaking Foldable (Outside) 168
42B. Notetaking Foldable (Inside) 169
42C. Writing to Learn: Notetaking Foldable 171
43. Writing to Learn: Processing Information Boxes 174
44. Writing to Learn: Daily Reflections 176
45. Writing Poetry 178
46. Writing to Learn: The Power of Three 180
47. Writing to Learn: Facts vs. Opinions 183
48. Writing a Memo for Communication 185
49. Writing an E-mail for Communication 187
50A. Writing to Learn: Writing a Want Ad 190
50B. Writing to Learn: Writing a Want Ad for a Specific Job 191
51. Writing to Learn: Say It with Pictures 193
52. Writing a Friendly Letter to a Pen Pal 197
53. Letter to Next Year's Class 199
54. Formal Writing Checklist 201
55A. Writing Plan—Formal Writing: Persuasion/Argumentation 204
55B. Writer's Circle: Peer Editing 207
56. Formula for Writing for a Timed Essay Writing Test 209
57. Writing to Learn: Writing for a Younger Audience 212
58. Writing to Learn: Paraphrasing 214
59. Writing: Summarizing 217
60. Writing a Letter of Self-Evaluation 219

Preface

The purpose of this book is to offer teachers a resource that contains reading, writing, affective, cooperative, and best practices activities for all content areas. Since much of the text that teachers ask students to read is written above their instructional or independent reading level, students need strategies, skills, and practice to help them gain understanding of the material that they are expected to read and understand in all disciplines. Teachers tend to be experts in their own teaching fields and are quite adept at reading and teaching those subjects. However, in every class there are a wide range of readers, various degrees of motivation among students, and different levels of writing skill. I have found that teachers appreciate finding alternatives to help their students learn in a variety of ways. Once teachers and students experience success with a new idea, they are willing to repeat the strategy, skill, or activity again and again.

This book offers more than 60 activities on reading to learn and writing to learn, including lessons geared to accommodate different learning styles, a range of reading abilities, and various levels of motivation. Students need to feel comfortable and safe to want to learn; this area is the affective domain of teaching and learning. Several activities in this book will motivate students and help them connect to one another so the class can function as a team. Extensive research in the field of reading makes it quite clear that both reading and writing are processes, and both processes are necessary for learning. Reading improves writing, and writing improves reading.

Since the cognitive, affective, reading, and writing processes are all intertwined in the learning process, the activities in this book are organized in three sections, based on the major focus of the activities, with 20 activities in each section. Part 1 contains reading to learn activities; part 2 reading and writing to learn activities involving affective and cooperative learning; and part 3 writing to learn activities. Within each activity are suggestions for continued guided practice. Best practices suggest that teachers model first, then offer guided practice, and finally lead students to independence.

All the activities and lessons in the book have been successfully used at various grade levels in all content areas. I have taught all grades in more than thirty years of teaching and am currently teaching high school and conducting workshops with content teachers, and as a result all of the ideas have been used, evaluated, changed, and shared with other colleagues. My most challenging and rewarding students have been those who walked into my classes as nonreaders and nonwriters and left as motivated readers and writers as well as lifelong learners.

I have been fortunate to work with and to learn from some very talented educators, who have been willing to share their expertise and model great teaching. This book allows me to share some of my "best" teaching ideas with others. All learners appreciate choice and variety in learning. I hope that this book of ideas offers your students success both in their reading and writing, to increase their ownership of learning.

Introduction

I developed this book as a resource for teachers to use to improve student learning based on current research in best practices for classroom instruction and learning strategies. In all the activities, good teaching involves doing the following: Model the lesson first and teach a mini lesson if necessary, then provide guided practice in groups or pairs, then move students toward independence. All of the activities have been used in real classrooms by teachers in various content areas at various grade levels. Students need to interact with text actively and be able to write about their learning, no matter what the subject or grade level is. The basic premise of this book, based on research, is that reading and writing are interconnected processes and reading improves writing and writing improves reading. If one process is neglected then the other suffers as well.

Current reading researchers such as Ellin Keene (Keene and Limmermann 1997), Stephanie Harvey (Harvey and Goudvis 2000), Timothy Shanahan (Tierney and Shanahan 1991), and others, agree that there are basic habits or skills that increase comprehension and learning in all content areas. This is the focus of part 1, "Reading to Learn," which contains 20 activities. Each activity includes an explanation of the activity and how to use it, plus a number of handouts (43 in this section) for students to use in the activities. The comprehension skill areas covered are previewing, asking questions, finding main ideas, using vocabulary, visualizing, making inferences, monitoring, connecting to text, synthesizing, and practicing fluency.

In addition, many of the activities include the practices of cooperative learning established by Johnson and Johnson (1989), which engage students and reinforce "interdependence" while working in teams. Research-based strategies of classroom instruction drawn from Robert Marzano's (2004) work are the foundation of the activities in this book. His research suggests nine categories of strategies that improve student learning: (1) identifying similarities and differences, (2) summarizing and notetaking, (3) reinforcing effort and providing recognition, (4) doing homework and practicing, (5) nonlinguistic representations, (6) cooperative learning, (7) setting objectives, (8) providing feedback, and (9) generating and testing hypotheses.

In addition, I based the activities on brain-based learning on the research of David Sousa (2006), and Eric Jensen (2005). Their work seems to agree that students need active, meaningful learning; accurate, helpful feedback; a rich, stimulating environment; and a safe environment: this is the affective domain. Students need to feel comfortable in order to pay attention and focus on learning. This area is the focus of the 20 activities in part 2, "Reading and Writing to Learn Involving Affective and Cooperative Learning." These activities each also include an explanation of the activity and how to use it, as well as handouts (25 in this section) for students to use.

In the area of writing, Harvey Daniels (2007) and William Strong (2006) are two experts who promote the necessity of having students "write to learn" to increase processing, connecting, and ownership of learning. In part 3, "Writing to Learn," the 20 activities are designed to engage students in writing to process information, do authentic writing, and practice formal writing. They also include explanatory material and handouts for students (24 in this section).

A major goal for teachers is to have students become lifelong readers, writers, and learners. To accomplish this goal, students need strategies and practice to achieve ownership of their learning. With high-stakes tests facing both teachers and students, this book will empower both and be a practical resource in any content area.

For literacy coaches or staff developers, the strategies and activities can be shared with content teachers to promote reading and writing within the curriculum. Once teachers experience success with a strategy, technique, or lesson, they, like their students, will improve and use it again. Although teachers are experts in their content areas, the wide range of students' abilities makes teaching more and more challenging. The literacy coach can use this book as a resource for ideas to use with teachers to improve student learning in the classroom.

Part 1

Reading to Learn

Activity 1

Reading to Learn (Pre- or Post-): Content Continuum

Purpose of the Activity

The purpose of this activity is for teachers and students to preview the knowledge and concepts of a unit or lesson. The students are directed to make choices based on their background knowledge, former experiences, and values structure and to defend their choices orally, with details.

How to Use the Activity

After duplicating and distributing handouts 1B and 1D or creating a continuum on large poster paper, have students write opposing concepts, viewpoints, or feelings at each end of the arrows. The two discussion statements should be based on the main ideas of the reading selection or content of the unit. (Handouts1A and 1C contain examples of discussion statements; more are listed below.) Statements should be placed at the top and the bottom of the vertical arrows. If there are more than one set of statements and several continuums, Post the continuums in the four corners of the room. Place statements about the content unit that may be controversial or opposing conceptual statements on the continuums for the students to critically think about and take a position on, using the sticky dots. Students will need a sticky dot for each continuum. For accountability, ask students be to write their initials on each dot. After previewing the statements and explaining the activity, ask students to walk around the room and place one colored sticky dot on the vertical line of each continuum.

After all students have completed the task, follow up by asking randomly chosen students to explain why they placed their dots where they did. Also, ask students to note any patterns of the placement of the dots.

At the end of the unit, use the activity again with the same set of statements and different colored dots so the teacher can see changes in opinion, growth of knowledge, or personal insights.

Examples of discussion statements:

- The North is responsible for the Civil War/The South is responsible for the Civil War.

- Textbooks are easier to read and comprehend than they used to be./Textbooks are harder to read and comprehend than they used to be.

- The more one reads, the better reader one becomes./How much one reads has no effect on one how well one reads.

Use handouts 1C and 1D at the beginning of a course or during a discussion on reading. Students are asked to critically think about the statements and make a choice based on their own background knowledge about reading and writing problems. Each student *must* place one dot by one choice. (This is not optional.) Discuss the answers with the whole class and provide an explanation for each choice. The multiple choice format offers another continuum for a whole class activity for asking questions about content as a preview or a review for a test. One or several multiple choice continuums can be used at the same time in the classroom.

Evaluation

This activity can be given a participation grade or simply used as a previewing, motivational activity. The cognitive and affective growth will not be realized until the end of the unit, when the activity is revisited or there is a more formal assessment.

Variation(s)

Another possibility is to use the activity after a reading. By using a continuum at both the beginning and end of the lesson or unit, the teacher and the students can easily see changes in opinion; growth in knowledge; and affective connections to a philosophical idea, content concept, or affective mindset.

1A. CONTINUUM

Reading and writing are essential to my learning.

1B. CONTINUUM

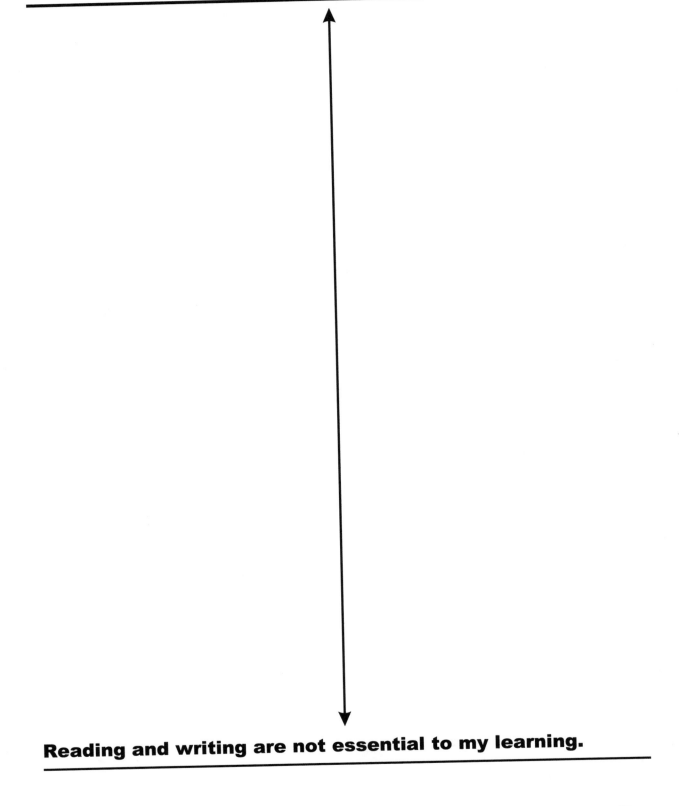

Reading and writing are not essential to my learning.

1C. PLACE A DOT BY WHAT YOU CONSIDER TO BE THE MOST IMPORTANT FACTOR CONTRIBUTING TO STUDENTS' INABILITY TO READ AND WRITE WELL.

A. Lack of training in the "basics," such as spelling, phonics, and grammar

B. Too much time in front of a TV, computer, or other video screen

C. Lack of parental support

D. Lack of knowledge of strategies they can apply

E. Too little time spent reading

F. Not enough practice at school

From *Reading and Writing to Learn: Strategies across the Curriculum* by Katherine Kuta. Westport, CT: Teacher Ideas Press. Copyright © 2008.

1D. PLACE A DOT BY WHAT YOU CONSIDER TO BE THE MOST IMPORTANT CONCEPT OF THIS UNIT THAT YOU KNOW THE MOST ABOUT FROM YOUR BACKGROUND KNOWLEDGE OR YOUR READING ABOUT THE TOPIC.

Course: _____

_____

Title of Unit: _____

_____

A. _____

_____

B. _____

_____

C. _____

_____

D. _____

_____

E. _____

_____

F. _____

_____

Activity 2

Previewing: Text Chapter, Magazine, and Newspaper

Purpose of the Activity

The purpose of this activity is for students to practice their previewing skills with a text chapter, magazine titles, and newspaper articles by completing a scavenger hunt. Students will become more aware of various periodicals that are available in the library as well as of periodicals that cover the content area being studied. Students will also think about the specific strategies involved in previewing content material, an assignment, or pleasure reading material. Finally, students will read one article of interest and focus on the differences between facts and opinions. Handout 2C will help students become more familiar with the parts of a newspaper as well as practicing scanning and skimming skills.

How to Use the Activity

Use handout 2A to model and to guide students in previewing a textbook reading. The questions direct students to the unique text features of the reading so that they will increase their understanding of the content. Through repeated practice, using the previewing strategy becomes an automatic comprehension habit.

Schedule the class in the school library to use handout 2B. Students will have an opportunity to peruse the many titles available The activity will probably require an entire class period, because students will be asked to choose an article to read. By reading for the purpose of finding opinions and facts, the students will be reviewing an important skill. Note that an opinion is the thesis of an article or may be a quotation used for support, and facts are provable, supporting details. Ask students to share their findings. Students will share the title of a magazine that they did not know existed as well as something they learned from the reading. Another suggestion is to process the activity by talking about the strategies that are involved in choosing a book or magazine, such as reading the title, looking at the pictures, scanning the headline titles on the cover, skimming through the table of contents, flipping through the pages, thinking about the topics available, and connecting to prior experiences and knowledge. Point out to students the boldfaced verbs in handout 2B, which ask for specific tasks to be done. The goal is for students to make previewing an automatic habit in all their reading.

For handout 2C, the newspaper exercise, have students work in pairs or individually, depending on the number of newspapers available. The questions are generic, so any newspaper may be used. Questions could be changed to focus on more specific information if desired. For motivation, the activity could become a game: The first three people to finish could receive extra points. Answers may be discussed once everyone is done.

Evaluation

This activity should be counted as a class activity and be given the appropriate credit for completion and participation.

Variation(s)

This activity can be used in the classroom or in the library. If there is a large variety of magazines in the classroom, students may complete this activity there. Another possibility is to substitute newspapers for magazines in the previewing exercise. This activity will give students a chance to preview several newspaper formats.

In handout 2C, to ensure greater success, the sections and page numbers may be filled in for students if their skills are low or they are English as a second language learners.

2A. PREVIEWING A TEXTBOOK READING

Name: _____

Directions: This activity is designed to help you look over the chapter to be read and studied. Remember that previewing means looking over and thinking about what you know and what you want to know about the topic.

Topic: _____

Chapter Title or Title of Reading: _____

Pages: _____

1. What is the largest and darkest print on the first page of the reading?

2. Write 5 things that you may already know about the topic.

3. List 5 words and/or ideas that you think will be included in the reading.

4. List 5 photos, graphs, or other visuals that appeal to your eye as you page through the reading.

5. If there are any boldface, dark headings in the reading, write 5 of them here.

6. If there are any boldface, dark vocabulary terms in the reading, write 5 of them here.

7. Look for additional information in the reading, such as questions, objectives, a summary, or other information. List and explain the purpose of each.

8. What is one interesting visual, word, fact, or question that stands out in this reading?

9. What did you learn by doing this activity?

10. Why is previewing an important reading strategy?

Draw a picture that best represents this reading based on your previewing today.

From *Reading and Writing to Learn: Strategies across the Curriculum* by Katherine Kuta. Westport, CT: Teacher Ideas Press. Copyright © 2008.

2B. PREVIEWING MAGAZINES AND READING TO LEARN

Name: _____

Directions: Because many libraries subscribe to more than 50 periodicals, the goal of this activity is for you to become more familiar with current magazines and to help you find magazines of particular interest to you.

1. **Brainstorm:** Think of as many magazine titles as you can and list them on the back of this sheet.

2. **Preview and list** the titles of 3 magazines that you have looked at or read before today.

3. **Scan** various unfamiliar magazines that you may not have realized existed and record 10 new titles.

   1.   6.
   2.   7.
   3.   8.
   4.   9.
   5.   10.

4. **Choose** 1 magazine that looks the most interesting to you and **explain** why you might want to read it again.

   Title: _____
   Why? _____
   Why did you choose this one?_____
   _____

5. **Skim** the table of contents and **choose** 1 article from the magazine, **read** it, and **write** your opinion of the article as well as 5 facts that you learned.

   Title: _____
   Pages: _____
   Author: _____
   Opinion: _____
   _____

Facts: What is a fact? _____
1.
2.
3.
4.
5.

2C. PREVIEWING A NEWSPAPER: SCAVENGER HUNT

Name: _____

Directions: The purpose of this activity is for you to become familiar with all parts of a newspaper, which supplies current events and information to the public. Record your answers as well as the section and page numbers.

Title of Newspaper: _____

Date of Issue: _____

1. For how many years has the paper been published? _____

2. What is the "headline news" or largest print on the front page? _____

   _____

3. What is one of the picture illustrations on the front page? _____

   _____

4. How many sections does the newspaper contain today? _____

5. What is the phone number of the newspaper? _____

6. What is one "world or international" news story headline? _____

7. What is one "national" news story headline? _____

8. Name 3 countries that are in the news in this issue: _____

   _____

   _____

9. What is one "local" news story in the news in this issue? _____

   _____

   _____

10. Name 3 people who are in the news in this issue: _____

    _____

    _____

(1 of 2)

From *Reading and Writing to Learn: Strategies across the Curriculum* by Katherine Kuta. Westport, CT: Teacher Ideas Press. Copyright © 2008.

11. What is the high and low temperature in Honolulu, Hawaii? _____

12. How many people are listed in the "Obituary" or Death Notice section? _____

13. Name 3 advertisements that are full-page ads: _____

_____

_____

14. What is the title of one feature (human interest story) in this issue? _____

_____

15. What TV show is on tonight at 9:00 P.M. on WGN? _____

16. What movie is playing that looks interesting at the nearest movie theater to you?

_____

17. Name 3 sports players who are in this issue: _____

_____

18. What is your horoscope sign, and what does it mean (in your own words)? _____

_____

_____

19. What is one kind of animal that is for sale in the classified section? _____

20. Name one fact that is on the last page of the newspaper: _____

_____

What did you learn from doing this activity? _____

_____

_____

(2 of 2)

From *Reading and Writing to Learn: Strategies across the Curriculum* by Katherine Kuta. Westport, CT: Teacher Ideas Press. Copyright © 2008.

Activity 3

Previewing, Scanning, and Skimming

Purpose of the Activity

There are several purposes for the three parts of this "during reading" activity, which may be used as one lesson or as three separate ones. Handout 3A offers students practice in previewing a chapter of their textbook by scanning through the pages to observe, locate, and record specific key words, illustrations, and features of the text. Handout 2B asks students to practice their questioning and skimming skills by having them write their own questions based on the headings, boldface words, and illustrations and skim to find the answers to their questions as a preview to reading the text. Students will learn to create their own purpose for reading the textbook. Handout 2C helps students practice the scanning and skimming skills necessary for research on the Internet: asking a question, locating an appropriate Web site, scanning for key words, and skimming for information. Finally, students will monitor and evaluate their own learning. These skills are necessary for both classroom reading and state test reading. Students need to learn to adjust their reading according to the purpose, type of text, and comprehension level goal. They should realize that the speed and concentration level of their reading can affect their comprehension of the text. Generally, the faster they read, the lower their comprehension level is.

How to Use the Activity

These activities may be used in any content area with informational text. Since reading rate is often overlooked or assumed in content classes, students tend to read everything at one rate, which is usually fast, and they do not always read for a purpose (except to get done). The rates of reading may be taught as a mini-lesson, and the students should be tested to determine their individual words-per-minute rate using any timed reading book. Students often are interested in and motivated to find out their individual scores.

Because previewing improves comprehension, this activity gives students extended practice at using scanning to preview a chapter or a section of informational text. Model this activity to the whole group to familiarize students with the structure of the specific book being taught. Students may also work in pairs to ensure the success of the activity. The handouts may be modified to meet the needs of the students or the format of the text being studied.

Use the scanning exercise in handout 3A repeatedly so that students will eventually use the skill of previewing automatically. The questions direct the students' eyes to the key features of the reading, such as size of font; boldface or italics; and placement of text, the written concepts, and the visual illustrations, which graphically display the reading's concepts.

Use the skimming exercise in handout 3B as a follow-up to handout 2A to have students practice writing their own questions, reading for a purpose, and skimming for specific important information; this will vary with the structure of the text and the teacher's instructions. To have students read at a slower rate for a higher level of comprehension, have the students use two-column notetaking rather than just skimming for main ideas and an overview.

Use the scanning and skimming exercise in handout 3C for viewing a particular piece of text from the Internet or as practice for a research project in any content area. This activity gives students a chance to slowly go through the process of researching, scanning, and skimming. With so many factors and skills involved in researching, students should move deliberately, step-by-step through the process, including quoting, paraphrasing, and summarizing.

Evaluation

The activities may be assessed for classroom participation, cooperative learning, and completion. As always, by reflecting and commenting on their own learning, students are monitoring that learning.

Variation(s)

The students can be asked to practice their scanning and skimming skills with the local newspaper by asking them to do a scavenger hunt for specific information by scanning and skimming some articles for the 5 Ws in news articles or periodicals.

3A. SCANNING AND SKIMMING A CHAPTER

Name: _____

Directions: For this previewing and reading exercise, practice different reading rate skills.

1. Use your **scanning** skills to locate specific pieces of information in the chapter pages assigned, to get the "big picture" and overview of the concepts.

2. Then create questions about the concepts in order to read for a purpose while **skimming** the text. Read only the major points. You will have only 50% comprehension of the text. In other words, you will read to get only the gist of the chapter.

Chapter: _____

Pages: _____

Scanning to Preview: Locating Information

1. What is the largest and boldest type on the first page of the reading? (Copy the exact words.)
    _____
    _____

2. What is the key word, sometimes in boldface, dark print, on the first page of the reading?
    _____

3. What is the 1 illustration that stands out on the first page?
    _____

4. What are the objectives on the first page, if stated? Put them in your own words.
    _____
    _____
    _____

5. What are the boldface words, concept nouns, dates, or illustrations that stand out on every page of the reading? List the information, with the page number next to it. There should be *at least* 2 items per page.
    _____
    _____
    _____

6. What kind of information is at the end of the chapter or reading?
    _____

7. How many questions are at the end of the reading, if any? _____

8. Scan for 3 words, dates, or pictures that you have seen or heard of before and write them down.
    _____
    _____

9. What are the section headings? List them here.
    _____
    _____

10. What is the structure of the chapter, such as sequence, comparison/contrast, problem solution, or other?
    _____
    _____

From *Reading and Writing to Learn: Strategies across the Curriculum* by Katherine Kuta. Westport, CT: Teacher Ideas Press. Copyright © 2008.

3B. SKIMMING A CHAPTER

Name: _____

Directions: After completing the scanning activity, practice skimming for information. Using the information from the previous activity, read for the purpose of getting an overview of the concepts found in the reading.

Create questions based on the section titles, boldface words, and illustrations listed on handout 3A, using the **5 Ws: Who, What, What, Where,** and **Why,** plus **How.** Use the pattern below as a guide. After writing each question, skim to answer the question. There should be a minimum of 10 questions and 10 answers.

Title of Chapter :_____ **Pages:** _____

Develop questions using the text features listed:
    Illustrations
    Boldface, enlarged, or italicized words
    Section headings

1. Question _____

_____

Answer: _____ Page_____

2. Question _____

_____

Answer: _____ Page_____

3. Question _____

_____

Answer: _____ Page_____

4. Question _____

_____

Answer: _____ Page_____

5. Question _____

_____

Answer: _____ Page_____

6. Question _____

_____

Answer: _____ Page_____

7. Question _____

_____

Answer: _____ Page_____

8. Question _____

_____

Answer: _____ Page_____

9. Question _____

_____

Answer: _____ Page_____

10. Question _____

_____

Answer: _____ Page_____

11. Write a summary of the skimming information in fewer than 10 sentences.

_____

_____

_____

_____

_____

12. What pages, sections, or concepts do you need to read more carefully again for further understanding?

_____

_____

_____

_____

(2 of 2)

From *Reading and Writing to Learn: Strategies across the Curriculum* by Katherine Kuta. Westport, CT: Teacher Ideas Press. Copyright © 2008.

19

3C. SCANNING AND SKIMMING ON THE INTERNET

Name: _____

Directions: Practice scanning and skimming information on the Internet for the purpose of researching for an assignment, finding the answer to a question, or finding specific information. First you must scan a Web site for appropriateness, relation to the topic, and validity. After you find a valid site, decide what is useful by skimming to locate topic-related information.

Write the Question of Interest: _____

_____

Scanning

1. What is the topic to be researched, in fewer than 5 words?

2. What is the purpose of the search?

3. What kinds of information are you interested in finding?

4. What are the key words you are using in the search?

5. How many sites did you find in the first search?

6. How can you change the key words to narrow down the search? (Remember to use your notes about Boolean searches, quotation marks, and plus and minus signs to narrow the topic.)

7. Scan through the retrieved hits to find a possible site that may be valid and appropriate based on the topic, URL, and author.

    Topic:
    URL:
    Author:
    Information about Author:

(1 of 2)

8. Why is a URL with the extensions .edu, .gov, or .mil probably a reputable site?

9. Scan and skim for at least 5 key words and phrases that make a reference to your question of interest.

10. Do you think that this site will add to your knowledge or quest for an answer to your question? Why or why not?

11. What is the exact Web address?

12. Skim the article or information piece for an answer to your question. Do the following:
    Find a direct quote:

    Write a paraphrase of a sentence:

    Write a summary of the text that gives you the information you need.

13. Write a short paragraph about the answer to your question.

14. What did you learn through doing this activity about scanning, skimming, and researching?

15. Why are different reading rates important? When should each of the following reading rates be used?
    Scanning
    Skimming
    Average rate
    Slowest rate

16. If directed, print the first page of the Web site and attach it to this activity sheet.

(2 of 2)

From *Reading and Writing to Learn: Strategies across the Curriculum* by Katherine Kuta. Westport, CT: Teacher Ideas Press. Copyright © 2008.

Activity 4

Asking Questions to Find the
Main Idea and Details

Purpose of the Activity

The purpose of this reading and writing activity is to have students practice developing their own questions using the boldface headings in an article or the section headings in a chapter of a textbook. By writing their own questions, reading for a purpose, writing the answers to the questions in their own words, and recording details to support the ideas, students practice reading for a purpose. This activity allows students to take ownership of their own reading as well as enabling them to read for deeper meaning to increase comprehension.

How to Use the Activity

Duplicate handout 4A for each major section of a chapter so that the information is in manageable portions for students to read and learn. Another option is to use the handout as a template for notetaking in their content notebooks. Model the strategy with the class as a whole group by creating questions based on the headings and displaying the questions on an overhead or LCD projector. Then ask students to read the first couple of sections, individually or in pairs. Discuss the process of summarizing the main ideas into succinct, everyday language. Have students take notes. During the next phase, have students work in pairs on assigned sections of text. If the students' skills warrant, assign them sections to work on individually.

For handout 4B, ask students to write one or more questions of each type based on the content. These will be "exit slips"; completion of the activity is necessary for a student to leave the room. The students' questions may be shared and discussed in the next class meeting.

Have students use handout 4C to create a one-page informational sheet on an assigned topic, section of text, article, biography, or other nonfiction reading. By restricting the information to one page, students learn to express main ideas in a few key words and phrases. Ask students to share the information with class members so that they will both teach and learn from one another.

Evaluation

These activities may be counted as a class or homework activity. Walk around the room to see whether students have completed the task of notetaking. It will be obvious through class discussion and sharing if students comprehend the reading.

Variation(s)

If the purpose of the reading is to have students answer the questions at the end of the chapter, then the students need to preview the questions before they read the material. One suggestion is to assign certain questions from the end of the chapter and ask students to record them in the left column of handout 4A. It is necessary for students to realize that some questions are literal and some are implicit or involve inferences, so one idea is to require the students to use two different colored highlighters for the two kinds of questions. Students will read for the answers to the explicit questions, "who," "what," "when," and "where". For the implicit questions, the students should answer "how," "why," and "what if". The students must use the textual information as well as their own background experiences and knowledge to answer the implicit questions.

Name: _____

Reading for Main Ideas

Title of Reading: _____

Pages: _____

Questions from Headings	Main Ideas	Important Details

Summary

Name: _____

Writing Questions to Learn

Thin Questions =
Literal = Explicit = in the Book
Ask: Who? What?? When?? Where???

Chubby Questions =
Inferences = Implicit = Critical Thinking = in Book and Head
Ask: Why? How?? What If???

4C. MAIN IDEAS: INFORMATIONAL PAGE TO SHARE

Topic: _____

Name: _____

Date: _____

Class: _____

Who or What?   Picture   When?

Why?   How?   When?

Connection   Memory Cue   Class Needs to Know

Sources:

Activity 5

Vocabulary Mapping

Purpose of the Activity

The purpose of this activity is to increase students' comprehension of concept vocabulary. Students need to interact with words often and in many different ways to commit them to long-term memory. They need to understand that the way a word is used determines the part of speech it is functioning as. Using picture memory cues for words increases connections and visualization comprehension.

How to Use the Activity

Use this vocabulary mapping exercise in conjunction with most of the other activities in this book and with both fiction and nonfiction. Words may be either assigned or self-selected. Learning is increased when students do the teaching, so have students present their vocabulary maps orally. Assign several students to present every day, and display the vocabulary maps in the classroom .Require class members to take notes to use for later study.

Model the activity first as a whole group, or present one mini-lesson on parts of speech and another on prefixes, suffixes, and roots. Model the skill of and use guided practice with contextual clues to determine the meaning of a word in a sentence.

Evaluation

For assessment, assign points for the vocabulary map based on a rubric with emphasis on accuracy, completeness, visual attractiveness, and size (the maps must be large enough for class members to see when they are displayed). Points may also be given for the oral presentation part, for being prepared, speaking loud enough, speaking slowly, and speaking clearly.

Variation(s)

One variation is to have students use the Excel® program to record the vocabulary information shared by their peers, for future reference or testing. For memory cues, students would insert clipart into the document.

5. VOCABULARY MAPPING

Name: _____

Directions: For each vocabulary word, either assigned or self-selected, complete a vocabulary map to help you and your classmates learn and remember the word.

One- to Three-Word Synonym

Word

Part of Speech, Sentence from Text, and Page from Text

Page _____

Picture Memory Cue

Definition in Your Own Words

Your Own Sentence

Activity 6

Visualizing Yourself Using Reading and Writing in 10 to 15 Years

Purpose of the Activity

The purpose of this visualization exercise is to demonstrate the purpose for reading and writing in students' lives. Students need to have a purpose for doing, learning, reading, and writing, just as adults do. By predicting and making inferences about the future, students are connecting to the communication processes involved in learning. By drawing and then writing about themselves, students are connecting visually and kinesthetically to the task. Students then must express themselves in writing and orally when they are asked to share. The activity could be used at the beginning of a new course so that students will make connections, set goals, and have an opportunity to learn about each other.

How to Use the Activity

Use this activity at the beginning of a new semester, new course, or new year. Have students use colors and draw pictures of themselves on the handout large enough for all class members to see when they introduce themselves. For modeling, explain how reading and writing is a part of both personal and professional daily life. Direct students to use symbols, stick people, or images cut out of a magazine or printed from a Web site in their pictures to represent a job, career, or their personal life.

Plan on using the activity with students as part of introductory 15- to 30-second, semi-impromptu speeches about themselves. Some questions to ask students are

- What did you not get to do over the summer that you wanted to do?

- What are you hobbies, or activities that you do when you are not eating, sleeping, or attending school?

- What is your favorite book and/or author?

- What kind of writing do you like to do?

- Do you have any words of wisdom to pass on after all your years in school?

- What makes you different from other people in the class?

- What long-term goal do you have for your life?

Questions may be put on the board for students to make notes on before they present. Finally, have students share and explain their illustrations. Through the students' sharing, both you and they learn about each other, which increases motivation for learning.

Evaluation

This activity may be assessed as a class exercise, with a given number of points for participating, or in other words, an "A" for participating and "zero" for not participating For motivation, offer extra points if all students take part.

Variation(s)

In specific content areas, this activity can be more content directed. Instead of asking about reading and writing in 10 to 15 years, the directions could ask about using social studies, geography, geometry, business courses, chemistry, or any other subject in 10 to 15 years. Students may need to brainstorm first for ideas, do research, or work in pairs.

6. VISUALIZING: USING READING AND WRITING IN 10–15 YEARS

Name: _____

Directions: Think about the future and picture how you might use reading and writing in your life. Will you be working? Will you have a family? What will you be doing that will require reading and writing skills every day?

Draw a picture of yourself using these reading and writing skills and then explain your picture in 3 sentences. Use color, be creative, and make it large enough for the whole class to see when you hold it up.

Explain the picture: _____

_____

_____

_____

_____

From *Reading and Writing to Learn: Strategies across the Curriculum* by Katherine Kuta. Westport, CT: Teacher Ideas Press. Copyright © 2008.

Activity 7

Visualizing: Drawing to Remember

Purpose of the Activity

The purpose of this activity is to give students the opportunity to practice one of the deeper meaning structures that "good readers" do while reading. Good readers visualize pictures in their minds that help make the text seem real, as if they are seeing a movie. By thinking, using their senses, and making a picture of a specific scene, students are recalling details and visualizing them. In addition, students will focus on an event to which they may have a special connection, which may lead to further discussion. With enough practice and reinforcement, students will automatically use visualization when they read independently.

How to Use the Activity

As a preview to this activity, check students' observation skills in this fun way. Ask students to close their eyes and raise their hands if they can see a picture of an object being mentioned. For example, "Who knows the color of the paint in the walls in the classroom?"; "Who knows the color of my shoes today?"; "Who knows what is on the bulletin board?"; and "Who noticed how many cars were parked in front of the school today?" These are scenes and objects that students have seen many times. Make a connection to the real world by talking about the jobs that require observation and visualization, such as forensic investigation (CSI) teams.

Use markers or colored pencils for this activity. Because many poor readers do not visualize, and see only black or only see pictures in shades of gray, using colors will reinforce visualize imagery. Model the activity with the entire class first and then use it as guided practice in pairs. It is important to time the students so that they realize that a product is expected to be done in a timely manner. If students have trouble forming a picture in their minds, ask them to bring in a photo to help them remember details. The directions in the handout ask students to use all the senses, to help them be more aware of all five senses and not just rely on their eyes. You may easily identify student learning styles as you observe the senses each student prefers to use. Because the majority of students are visual learners, many will draw what they saw. Auditory learners may focus on the surrounding sounds of the scene, and kinesthetic learners may focus on what they touched, or even a particular object.

The most important part of the activity is the discussion, both in pairs and as a class, about the clues that students used to guess what the pictures show, as well as how visualization can increase their learning.

Evaluation

This activity may be counted as a class activity and include points for participation. The accuracy of the guesses is not important; drawing, analyzing, and discussion are the goals of the activity.

Variation(s)

This activity may be extended to use with fiction or nonfiction text. As students are reading a novel or textbook, ask them to stop and form a picture of the scene in a story, a battle in a social studies unit, a scientific discovery, a math word problem, or even a driver's education class.

7. VISUALIZING: DRAWING TO REMEMBER

Directions: Think of a scene, object, place, or situation about which you have just read. Imagine and picture yourself in that place, scene, or situation or with that object. **See** the sights and colors, **hear** the background noises, **smell** the aromas, **taste** the surroundings, **feel** the sensations. Try to form a picture in your mind.

- Draw a picture of the image in your mind, with as many details as possible.

- Join a partner and see if he or she can guess what your picture shows.

Name of Your Partner: _____

His or her guess: _____

What did your partner guess correctly? _____

_____

What were the clues that helped him or her guess? _____

_____

How can this strategy of visualizing an image improve your learning?

_____

_____

Activity 8

Symbolism on the Penny and the Dollar Bill

Purpose of the Activity

There are several purposes for this activity. The first is to have students practice their skills of observation by carefully looking at objects they are very familiar with, such as a penny or a dollar bill. Second, they must work in pairs and critically think about the meaning of the symbols used on the money. Third, students will visualize and create a new coin or dollar with new symbols and decide on specific placement on the coin and dollar, drawing their own currency. Finally, students must explain their choices in writing, to share with the class.

How to Use the Activity

One or all of the handouts may be used, depending on the purpose of the lesson. To prepare for the activity, obtain enough pennies for all students to work with, either individually or in pairs, on handouts 8A and 8B. Tell students to bring in their own dollar bills for handouts 8C and 8D.

For the first part of the activity, students may work in pairs or as individuals, observing details and thinking about symbolism, background knowledge, and the purpose of the lesson. If the students are struggling to answer the questions on handouts 8A and 8C, direct them to the Web sites listed on those handouts. Tell them to read for information so that they can complete the exercise.

For handouts 8B and 8D, the creative, critical thinking, writing part of the activity, students should work alone and draw a new coin or currency, and explain their choices. You may have students share their drawings and explanations with the class.

Answer key for handout 8C			
1, A	6, I	11,	D 16, L
2, H	7, J	12, Q	17, F
3, N	8, K	13, P	18, G
4, B	9, C	14, E	19, N
5, R	10, O	15, S	20, M

For handout 8D, tell students to be creative but also use their background knowledge to make appropriate choices of symbols for their new dollar bills.

Evaluation

Each part of the activity should count for a class participation grade as well as sharing in pairs.

Variation(s)

Students may be interested in finding out more about currencies, coins, and other paper legal tender, so a mini research project would be a good extension project as a follow-up. Students may write questions and then narrow them down to practice learning how to ask questions; research to find answers; and write the information in such a way that others can learn from their findings, such as in a one-page visual, PowerPoint® presentation, or one-page report.

8A. VISUALIZATION AND OBSERVATION OF A PENNY

Name: _____

Directions:

- Complete the "anticipation guide" and mark your responses "agree" or "disagree."

- Find a partner for the activity.

- Use a penny as a visual for this activity. You and a partner should record the observations you have made by carefully looking at the coin.

- Check your understanding about the "penny" by reading the information on *The History of the United States Penny in the 20th Century* at www.pennies.org/history/intro.html and/or The United States Mint Web site at www.usnmint.gov. Find 5 new interesting facts to write on this sheet and share with the class.

Anticipation Guide:

1. The word *penny* is derived from the British coin called a "pence".　　Agree or Disagree

2. Pennies have been minted since 1977.　　Agree or Disagree

3. Lincoln's image first appeared on the penny in 1909.　　Agree or Disagree

4. Over 300 billion one cent coins have been produced since it was first designed.　　Agree or Disagree

5. Today the penny's composition is 97.2% zinc and 2.5% copper.　　Agree or Disagree

Observations:

1. Which way is Lincoln facing? _____ _____

2. Which way are the people facing on other coins, such as a nickel?

_____

_____

3. What is the first motto that appeared on a coin? _____

_____

_____

4. What is the national motto that means, "One out of many"? _____

_____

_____

5. What is to the left and right of Lincoln? _____

(1 of 2)

From *Reading and Writing to Learn: Strategies across the Curriculum* by Katherine Kuta. Westport, CT: Teacher Ideas Press. Copyright © 2008.

6. What appears on the back of the coin to commemorate the 150th anniversary of Lincoln's birth?

_____

7. Who is the person on the back of the coin? _____

8. What is the year of the penny you are holding? _____

Extra credit

9. What appeared on the back of a penny before 1959? _____

10. Why is the word "liberty' on the coin? _____

_____

What are 5 more fun facts about money? Answer in complete sentences.

1. _____

_____

_____

_____

2. _____

_____

_____

_____

3. _____

_____

_____

_____

4. _____

_____

_____

_____

5. _____

_____

_____

_____

38 From *Reading and Writing to Learn: Strategies across the Curriculum* by Katherine Kuta. Westport, CT: Teacher Ideas Press. Copyright © 2008.

8B. VISUALIZATION: DESIGNING A COIN

Name: _____

Directions: Design a coin for a historical, famous, noteworthy, scientific, or everyday person and explain the symbols for the front and the back of the coin. Draw your design in the 2 circles.

(1 of 2)

8C. MAKING OBSERVATIONS AND UNDERSTANDING SYMBOLISM USING A DOLLAR BILL

Name: _____

Partner: _____

Directions: Using a dollar bill, make careful observations with a partner and match the symbols on the dollar bill with matching interpretations for the symbols found below Then check your answers on the Web site *Understanding the Design and Symbolism of the U.S. One Dollar Bill* at www.niehs.nih.gov/kids/triviadollar.htm, which is the National Institute of Environmental Health Sciences site, or visit the Department of the U.S. Treasury Web site at www.ustreas.gov/education.

Part 1: Observations

List as many symbols, numbers, and pictures that appear on the FRONT of the bill as possible.

List as many symbols, numbers, and pictures that appear on the BACK of the dollar bill as possible.

What items did you observe that you had not observed before you looked carefully at the dollar today?

Part 2: Matching symbols with meaning

For each item, print the letter of the description from the list below that matches it.

_____ 1. motto, "In God We Trust"

_____ 2. cotton and linen blend, with red and blue silk fibers

_____ 3. United States Treasury seal

_____ 4. balancing scales

_____ 5. 1776

_____ 6. key

_____ 7. two circles on back

(1 of 2)

From *Reading and Writing to Learn: Strategies across the Curriculum* by Katherine Kuta. Westport, CT: Teacher Ideas Press. Copyright © 2008.

_____ 8. pyramid

_____ 9. unfinished pyramid

_____ 10. all-seeing eye

_____ 11. *annuit coetis*

_____ 12. *novus ordo seclorum*

_____ 13. seal of the President of the United States

_____ 14. bald eagle

_____ 15. unsupported shield

_____ 16. *e pluribus unum*

_____ 17. above eagle: 13 stars

_____ 18. olive branch and arrows

_____ 19. number 13

_____ 20. George Washington

A. appeared on paper money for the first time in 1957

B. represents justice

C. possible meaning is "our country was not yet finished"

D. "God has favored our undertaking"

E. American origin

F. original colonies

G. power of peace and war

H. the paper dollar is really fabric

I. symbol of authority

J. two sides of the Great Seal of the United States

K. represents "strength and duration"

L. means "one nation from many people"

M. first president of the United States

N. represents repeatedly the beginning of the country

O. ancient symbol for divinity

P. the seal was approved in 1782

Q. a Latin phrase that is interpreted to mean "a new order for the world"

R. found at the base of the pyramid

S. the United States needs to rely on its own virtue

(2 of 2)

8D. CREATING YOUR OWN DOLLAR BILL

Name: _____

Directions: Think creatively and plan the symbols, layout, and colors for a new, appropriate dollar bill that commemorates an important person in history or modern society. You must have a central focus on an individual and use at least 5 symbols for the front and 5 symbols for the back of the bill. Each symbol must include an explanation. Use the back of this page to show the back of the bill.

Explanations of Choices Made:

Person in focus: _____

Why should this person be honored? (Write in complete sentences.)

_____

_____

_____

Symbols for front of dollar and explanation of what each object represents:

_____

_____

_____

_____

Symbols for back of dollar and explanation of what each object represents:

_____

_____

_____

_____

From *Reading and Writing to Learn: Strategies across the Curriculum* by Katherine Kuta. Westport, CT: Teacher Ideas Press. Copyright © 2008.

Activity 9

Inference: Hidden Meaning in Advertisements

Purpose of the Activity

The purpose of this activity is for students to practice the deeper meaning comprehension skill of making inferences while reading. Newspaper and magazine advertisements are readily available, so students can use the ads to observe the words, pictures, and propaganda devices that are used in marketing to convince and to sell products.

How to Use the Activity

Cut out newspaper and/or magazine advertisements ahead of time. Or have students choose their own ads to cut out for this activity; this would create more interest and motivation.

Model the activity as a whole class exercise in which the class makes observations and discusses the meaning of the advertisements. Then each group, pair, or individual should be responsible for completing a handout. Students may discuss their findings with other in small groups or with the entire class. Ask students to staple their ads to the worksheet.

Choose an ad that will appeal to teenagers for the class modeling. Have students record the company's name and the product or service being marketed on the back of handout 9. Ask them to write down the words and phrases in the ad. Discuss the denotations and connotations of the words. Have students observe and record the literal visual images and the implied messages of the symbols. Discuss the type of consumer the ad might appeal to. Take a poll of the class and record who would be interested in the product or service based on this ad.

Evaluation

This may be graded as a class activity for participation, cooperation, and completion of the activity. Students may also be given points for sharing with others.

Variation(s)

Ask students to find ads that appeal to a variety of audiences, such as adults, teenagers, children, the elderly, the wealthy, or other population groups.

This activity may also use ads that focus on a particular holiday, such as Valentine's Day. Direct students to the change of focus, to romance, feelings, and couples in the advertising. Students may make a list of the symbols, pictures, ad models, and use of color in the ads and why they think these were chosen.

9. INFERENCING: FINDING THE HIDDEN MESSAGES IN ADVERTISEMENTS

Name: _____

Directions: Cut out 2 ads from the newspaper. Make sure each ad has both pictures and words. Then complete the organizer below and attach the ads to the back of this sheet.

Title of Newspaper (underline title): _____

Date of Paper: _____

AD 1

Section and page: _____

Product, company, or service being marketed: _____

Words used in ad: _____

_____

_____

_____

What is the meaning being conveyed by the words? _____

_____

_____

What are the visuals? _____

_____

_____

What is the meaning being conveyed by the images? _____

_____

_____

Whom is the ad appealing to in society? _____

_____

_____

What inferences can you make from the ad that are not directly stated? _____

_____

_____

Does the ad make you want to buy or use the product? Why or why not? _____

_____

_____

(1 of 2)

AD 2

Section and page: _____

Product, company, or service being marketed: _____

Words used in ad: _____

_____

_____

_____

What is the meaning being conveyed by the words? _____

_____

_____

What are the visuals? _____

_____

_____

What is the meaning being conveyed by the images? _____

_____

_____

Whom is the ad appealing to in society? _____

_____

_____

What inferences can you make from the ad that are not directly stated? _____

_____

_____

Does the ad make you want to buy or use the product? Why or why not? _____

_____

_____

Activity 10

Inference Practice with Literacy Quotations

Purpose of the Activity

This cooperative pairing activity has students practice several skills. First, students practice fluency by reading the quote aloud while looking for the partner with the same quote. Next, students discuss the implied meaning of the quote by examining the writer's choice of words to communicate a message. Then students work cooperatively to complete the activity handout. Students will also discuss connections between the meaning of the literacy quote and their own lives, other texts, or the world. Finally, students will search for additional famous quotations and write their own literacy statements.

How to Use the Activity

This activity may be used at any time with any subject, but it is desirable to use it at the beginning of a period or school day, because after completing it students will be in groups and affectively connected so they can work together on a content activity. By reading, discussing, inferring, connecting, and writing, students are practicing several deep meaning structures that improve long-term comprehension. This activity can be timed for 15 minutes individually or can be discussed with the entire class if the purpose is to reinforce any of these skills.

Evaluation

Depending on the purpose of the activity, the quotations (handouts 10A and 10C) may be used for pairing, with or without handout 10B, for a class grade.

Variation(s)

The strategy of pairing by using famous quotations could be used with quotations about any particular subject or content unit. Students could also be asked to bring in quotes.

Another possibility is to ask students to write their own quotations about a particular concept being studied. Often the quotations will involve similes, metaphors, or other figures of speech, which require critical thinking.

10A. INFERENCE PRACTICE WITH LITERARY QUOTATIONS

Name: _____

Partner: _____

Find the Partner with the Same Reading Quote

Directions: After finding the partner who has the same quote, discuss the meaning of the quote and why it is an important statement about literacy. Also try to think of a connection between the message and your own lives.

"Books are the best bridges I have ever crossed." Nancy White Carlstrom	"Books are the best bridges I have ever crossed." Nancy White Carlstrom
"Libraries and books have changed my life—they have made it possible." Myra Cohn Livingston	"Libraries and books have changed my life—they have made it possible." Myra Cohn Livingston
"Reading is to the mind, what exercise is to the body." Addison	"Reading is to the mind, what exercise is to the body." Addison
"In science, read, by preference, the newest works; in literature, the oldest. The classic literature is always modern." Bulwer-Lytton	"In science, read, by preference, the newest works; in literature, the oldest. The classic literature is always modern." Bulwer-Lytton
"When I am reading a book whether wise or silly, it seems to me to be alive and talking to me." Jonathan Swift	"When I am reading a book whether wise or silly, it seems to me to be alive and talking to me." Jonathan Swift
"I have never read to change my life but to find new lives. (There are never enough.)" Elizabeth Fitzgerald Howard	"I have never read to change my life but to find new lives. (There are never enough.)" Elizabeth Fitzgerald Howard
"Let us read and let us dance—two amusements that will never do any harm to the world." Voltaire	"Let us read and let us dance—two amusements that will never do any harm to the world." Voltaire

(1 of 3)

 From *Reading and Writing to Learn: Strategies across the Curriculum* by Katherine Kuta. Westport, CT: Teacher Ideas Press. Copyright © 2008.

"Through reading I learned to journey out of myself and back again, but on the return voyage I brought riches and power in the form of thoughts to last a lifetime." Anne Rockwell	"Through reading I learned to journey out of myself and back again, but on the return voyage I brought riches and power in the form of thoughts to last a lifetime." Anne Rockwell
"Books are not made for furniture, but there is nothing else so beautifully furnishes a house." Henry Ward Beecher	"Books are not made for furniture, but there is nothing else so beautifully furnishes a house." Henry Ward Beecher
"Force yourself to reflect on what you read, paragraph by paragraph." Samuel Taylor Coleridge	"Force yourself to reflect on what you read, paragraph by paragraph." Samuel Taylor Coleridge
"A good word is like a good tree whose root is firmly fixed and whose top is in the sky." The Koran	"A good word is like a good tree whose root is firmly fixed and whose top is in the sky." The Koran
"There is more treasure in books than in all the pirate's loot on Treasure Island." Walt Disney	"There is more treasure in books than in all the pirate's loot on Treasure Island." Walt Disney
"The more that you read, the more things you will know. The more that you learn, the more places you'll go." Dr. Seuss	"The more that you read, the more things you will know. The more that you learn, the more places you'll go." Dr. Seuss
"To read without reflecting is like eating without digesting." Edmund Burke	"To read without reflecting is like eating without digesting." Edmund Burke
"Words are the voice of the heart." Roger Ebert	"Words are the voice of the heart." Roger Ebert
"We read to know we are not alone." C. S. Lewis	"We read to know we are not alone." C. S. Lewis
"There is no friend as loyal as a book." Ernest Hemingway	"There is no friend as loyal as a book." Ernest Hemingway

From *Reading and Writing to Learn: Strategies across the Curriculum* by Katherine Kuta. Westport, CT: Teacher Ideas Press. Copyright © 2008.

"This will never be a civilized country until we expend more money for books than we do for chewing gum." **Elbert Hubbard**	"This will never be a civilized country until we expend more money for books than we do for chewing gum." **Elbert Hubbard**
"Beware the man of one book." **Saint Thomas Aquinas**	"Beware the man of one book." **Saint Thomas Aquinas**
"A classic is a book that has never finished saying what it has to say." **Italo Calvino**	"A classic is a book that has never finished saying what it has to say." **Italo Calvino**
"What one reads becomes part of what one sees and feels." **Ralph Ellison**	"What one reads becomes part of what one sees and feels." **Ralph Ellison**
"I find television very educating. Every time someone turns the set on, I go into the other room and read a book." **Groucho Marx**	"I find television very educating. Every time someone turns the set on, I go into the other room and read a book." **Groucho Marx**
"A book must be the ax for the frozen sea within us." **Franz Kafka**	"A book must be the ax for the frozen sea within us." **Franz Kafka**
"Reading furnishes the mind only with materials of knowledge. It is thinking that makes what we read ours." **John Locke**	"Reading furnishes the mind only with materials of knowledge. It is thinking that makes what we read ours." **John Locke**
"A great book should leave you with many experiences, and slightly exhausted at the end. You live several lives while reading it." **William Styron**	"A great book should leave you with many experiences, and slightly exhausted at the end. You live several lives while reading it." **William Styron**
"The palest ink is clearer than the best memory." **Eugene Webb**	"The palest ink is clearer than the best memory." **Eugene Webb**
"I never met a book I didn't like." **Thomas Jefferson**	"I never met a book I didn't like." **Thomas Jefferson**

10B. DISCUSSION SHEET: INFERENCING

Name: _____

Partner's Name: _____

Using a Quote to Practice Inferencing

1. State the quote and the author:

_____

_____

_____

_____

2. Explain the unstated meaning of the quote (inference):

_____

_____

_____

_____

3. Explain the clues in the quote, such as words and phrases, that suggest the additional meaning.

_____

_____

_____

_____

4. Explain the connections of the quote to your lives.

_____

_____

_____

_____

5. Write an original sentence about literacy that you and your partner think is worth repeating to others.

_____

_____

_____

_____

Extra credit: Find an additional quote on literacy and "read between the lines" for the inferences involved.

_____

_____

_____

_____

10C. MAKING INFERENCES USING FAMOUS QUOTES

Name: _____

Famous Writing Quotes

Directions: Find the partner who has the same quote and discuss the meaning of and make an inference about the significance of the famous words.

Name: _____

Partner's name: _____

Quote: _____

_____

_____

_____

Author: _____

Meaning in your own words: _____

_____

_____

_____

Inference: _____

_____

_____

_____

Background on author: (Who, What, When, Where, and Why is this person important?)

_____

_____

_____

_____

(1 of 3)

Famous Writing Quotes

"The difference between fiction and reality? Fiction has to make sense." Tom Clancy	"The difference between fiction and reality? Fiction has to make sense." Tom Clancy
"Anyone can make history; only a great man can write it." Oscar Wilde	"Anyone can make history; only a great man can write it." Oscar Wilde
"Four hostile newspapers are more to be feared than a thousand bayonets." Napoleon Bonaparte	"Four hostile newspapers are more to be feared than a thousand bayonets." Napoleon Bonaparte
"No matter what you do, somebody always imputes meaning into your books." Theodor Seuss Geisel	"No matter what you do, somebody always imputes meaning into your books." Theodor Seuss Geisel
"I am the literary equivalent of a Big Mac and Fries." Stephen King	"I am the literary equivalent of a Big Mac and Fries." Stephen King
"My aim is to put down on paper, what I see and what I feel in the best and simplest way." Ernest Hemingway	"My aim is to put down on paper, what I see and what I feel in the best and simplest way." Ernest Hemingway
"Writing saved me from the sin and inconvenience of violence." Alice Walker	"Writing saved me from the sin and inconvenience of violence." Alice Walker

(2 of 3)

From *Reading and Writing to Learn: Strategies across the Curriculum* by Katherine Kuta. Westport, CT: Teacher Ideas Press. Copyright © 2008.

"Writing is not like painting, where you add. It is not what you put on the canvas that the reader sees. Writing is more like a sculpture, where you remove, you eliminate in order to make the work invisible. Even those pages you remove somehow remain." Elie Wiesel	"Writing is not like painting, where you add. It is not what you put on the canvas that the reader sees. Writing is more like a sculpture, where you remove, you eliminate in order to make the work invisible. Even those pages you remove somehow remain." Elie Wiesel
"A word is a bud attempting to become a twig. How can one not dream while writing? It is the pen which dreams. The blank page gives the right to dream." Gaston Bachelard	"A word is a bud attempting to become a twig. How can one not dream while writing? It is the pen which dreams. The blank page gives the right to dream." Gaston Bachelard
"Yes, it's hard to write, but it's harder not to." Carl Van Dorn	"Yes, it's hard to write, but it's harder not to." Carl Van Dorn
"Work on good prose has three steps: a musical stage when it is composed, and architectonic one when it is built, and a textile one when it is woven." Walter Benjamin	"Work on good prose has three steps: a musical stage when it is composed, and architectonic one when it is built, and a textile one when it is woven." Walter Benjamin
"All good writing is swimming under water and holding your breath." F. Scott Fitzgerald	"All good writing is swimming under water and holding your breath." F. Scott Fitzgerald
"What I like in a good author isn't what he says, but what he whispers." Logan Pearsall Smith	"What I like in a good author isn't what he says, but what he whispers." Logan Pearsall Smith

(3 of 3)

Activity 11

Making Inferences with Cartoons

Purpose of the Activity

The main purpose of this activity is to have students practice making inferences using cartoons, which usually contain the printed word and visuals. Making inferences involves using background information and thinking about the clues in the text to make educated guesses about meaning. Because state tests and the ACT reading test require students to be proficient in this skill while reading in a timed setting, students need to have extended practice with this deeper meaning comprehension skill.

There are several other purposes for this activity. Students will gain an understanding of the difference between literal or factual information and an inference or unstated information. As does all text, cartoons have a message or theme that the author is trying to convey, and students will gain further understanding of this important concept by using this genre. Students will also learn about irony, because much of the humor in cartoons is the result of something happening or being said that someone does not expect. Making predictions is a form of inference, and when asked to predict the next frame, students must make sense of the information in order to do so.

How to Use the Activity

Cartoons are readily available in newspapers, magazines, and books, and on the Internet, so students have easy access to a wide variety of current, political, topical, and content-oriented cartoons. Many students do not think that cartoons are funny because they do not understand them, so by learning how to analyze them, students' comfort level and understanding will increase.

Ask students to either choose a cartoon from a selected group of cartoons or locate a cartoon in the newspaper. The handout is appropriate for either option. As always, model one or more cartoons with the class and lead a whole group discussion, including all the questions on the handout. For guided practice, have students work together in pairs on one cartoon. When the comfort level is appropriate, ask students to work independently.

Students learn from each other, so ask them to share with each other or in groups of four or five and have them choose their favorite cartoon to share with the class. If a projection machine is available or the cartoon is online, display it for the entire class. Make sure to ask the students to explain both the word and visual clues that helped them reach the conclusions listed on their handouts.

Evaluation

This activity may be counted as a class, group, or individual class grade or homework grade based on completion, discussion, and sharing.

Variation(s)

One possibility is to ask students to draw the frames that would follow in the cartoon if they were employed as illustrators and asked to provide one to three more frames to fill out the space Students should then explain why they created the frames they did.

11. MAKING INFERENCES WITH CARTOONS

Name: _____

Directions: Use the skills of observation, critical thinking, and prediction to make inferences based on the cartoon provided.

Title of Cartoon: _____

Author: _____

Partner: _____

List 5 facts and/or literal details about the cartoon:

1. _____

2. _____

3. _____

4. _____

5. _____

What are the 3 inferences that you believe the author expects the reader to draw from reading "between the lines" to understand the cartoon?

1. _____

2. _____

3. _____

What is the point, message, or theme of the cartoon that is implied? (State in 1 sentence.)

What makes the cartoon funny or ironic?

What do you predict would happen next if you were to add an extra frame? Explain.

(1 of 2)

From *Reading and Writing to Learn: Strategies across the Curriculum* by Katherine Kuta. Westport, CT: Teacher Ideas Press. Copyright © 2008.

Imagine that the publisher asked you to create 3 more cartoon frames based on the cartoon. Draw the next 3 here.

(2 of 2)

Activity 12

Predicting and Making Inferences with Photos/Pictures

Purpose of the Activity

The primary purpose of this activity is for students to practice making observations and inferences based on photos and drawings. Students are asked to write an original caption and through their own inferences match captions to other visuals. Assessment is provided by asking students to write about their own learning process.

How to Use the Activity

Students will need access to newspapers and magazines that can be cut up for classroom use. Ask students to carefully examine several photos and captions, noting the length and the type of captions used in the newspaper or magazine they are viewing. Students could be paired up by using the handout for activity 21, the appointment clock. Students should join their partners, pick up a newspaper, scissors, glue, and a handout, listen to or read the directions, and begin the activity

First, students should locate one photo and caption, cut them out of the paper, and paste the pictures on the handout. They should place the captions on a table made available for all students to preview for part 2 of the handout. Partners will then exchange activity sheets, write an original caption to accompany their partner's photo, and explain the clues they used to decide what the caption should be.

In Part 2, ask students to peruse the captions and try to locate the original caption for their partner's picture. After they make their choice, they should paste it in the box on their handout and discuss their choice with their partners.

In Part 3, have students evaluate their own learning by thinking about photos, captions, and the need for visuals to increase communication.

Evaluation

This activity may be evaluated as a classroom activity for participation and cooperation with a partner. Points may be assigned for both areas.

Variation(s)

To encourage students to become more aware of the visuals in their textbooks, photocopy a page of content from the students' textbook that has both text and visuals. Cover the written portion of the page and duplicate it for the class. Ask students to write their own version of the text based on the visuals they see. For comparison, direct the students to the original page in their textbook. Remind students that visuals in a textbook are designed to visually display the same concepts that are expressed in written form on that page. Then discuss the students' observations and responses.

12. PREDICTING AND INFERRING WITH PHOTOS

Name: _____

Directions: After cutting out 1 newspaper or 1 magazine photo, along with its caption, paste the picture in the box below and turn in the caption to your teacher. Then exchange your worksheet with a partner. Each of you will write down what you think the caption should be for your partner's picture. Then look through the cut-out captions to find the original caption for that picture. Take it and paste it below the picture and explain why you think it is the original. Discuss your choices with your partner.

Paste Photo
Here

Part 1

Partner's name: _____

1. Write an original caption for the above picture here: _____

_____

2. What clues in the picture helped you make inferences?_____ _____

_____

Part 2

3. Paste the printed caption that you feel matches the picture here.

┌───┐
│   │
│   │
└───┘

4. Find the owner of the picture and ask if your guess was correct. Discuss your caption, the

inferred caption. _____

_____

_____

_____

6. Write 1 or 2 sentences about your guesses. Were they correct? Why or why not?

_____

_____

Part 3

7. What did you learn from this activity? Write 1 or 2 sentences explaining your answer.

_____

_____

_____

8. Why do you think photos, drawings, graphs, and other visuals are included in and

important to a newspaper or magazine? _____

_____

_____

Activity 13

Inferences: Visualizing and Illustrating Significant Quotes

Purpose of the Activity

Several of the deeper meaning structures of comprehension are practiced in this activity. Students are asked to find a quotation from the text that contains a main idea or an important detail to which they can connect. They are then asked to express their connection and the meaning of the quote in words as well as in picture form. This is a "during reading" activity, and it may be used with either fiction or nonfiction. By either reading for a significant quote or going back to the text to search for significant lines, students are involved in interacting with the text, re-reading it, evaluating its importance, and connecting to its ideas.

Students exhibit ownership of their learning by making personal choices and practice their verbal fluency by sharing with and learning from their classmates.

How to Use the Activity

This activity may be used as a class or homework activity. To model this activity, ask a student to suggest an important quote. Another possibility is to offer the students several quotes from which to choose one. Brainstorm for the meaning of the lines, for inferences from "reading between the lines," and for visual images. Then the entire class may draw their interpretations of the quote. For guided practice, students may work in pairs if the class needs more practice with these skills, before assigning independent practice.

When handing out the activity sheet and reading the directions, remind students that lines of text must be quoted exactly as written, and quotation marks must be placed both before and after the quotation. Students also need to take note of the page number and cite it correctly.

After the students have completed the writing and drawing, divide the students into groups to share quotes and illustrations, or ask individual students to share with the entire class. The handouts may also be displayed on the walls of the classroom.

Evaluation

Students may be given class participation points, completion points, and sharing points. Emphasis should be placed on stating significant lines, explaining their meaning, and displaying a visual.

Variation(s)

Place students in groups to choose the best quotations from the text, then place these placed on large poster paper for display and student use in formal writing in a subsequent lesson.

13. INFERENCES: SIGNIFICANT QUOTES

Name: _____

Finding Significant Lines in Text

Title of the Book: _____

Topic: _____

Directions: Choose the line(s) from the text that is/are the most significant to you. Write the line(s) below, putting the page number(s) in the parentheses at the end. Illustrate each choice(s) with a specific, sensory, visual example.

The line that is most significant to me is:

_____

_____

_____ (_____).

Explain the significance of the visual.

_____

_____

_____

_____

Activity 14

Making Inferences Using Visuals

Purpose of the Activity

The basic purpose of this activity is for students to interact with visuals and practice making inferences based on their observations, prior knowledge, and visual clues in the pictures. Each handout offers students practice with a different set of pictures, so they will draw conclusions based on a combination of pictures and clues. Handout 14A focuses on pictures of personal things, handout 14B on pictures of hobbies, handout 14C on pictures of behavioral traits, handout 14D on international driving signs, handout 14E on pictures of personal values, and handout 14F on classmates' objects and their values. The last two handouts offer extended writing opportunities for students to make generalizations, use details (the pictures) to support them, and conclude the writing with a summary.

How to Use the Activity

Begin with a mini-lesson on the skill of making inferences. Ask students to offer suggestions on when and where inferences—which involve making predictions, drawing conclusions, and making educated guesses—are used in the real world. Examples are riddles, artwork, meeting a person, looking at a photo album, seeing someone's house, viewing airport baggage, answering test questions, making choices, solving mysteries, and reading. Because inferences are based on clues and prior knowledge, use handouts 14A, 14B, 14C, and 14D as practice lessons in the classroom.

Use handout 14E for practice making inferences and also as a formal writing activity. Ask students to find and cut out six pictures that are representative of themselves and paste them in the boxes. Then have them write a generalization about themselves based on their choices. This generalization becomes their topic sentence and is supported with the explanation of the pictures in details within the paragraph. The ending sentence sums up and concludes the paragraph. (Refer handout 23C for a review of generalizations and details.)

Use handout 14F as an extension activity and ask each student to bring one object that they value to class. As each person shows the object and explains its value, class members should record what the object is and write an inference based on the "show and tell" by each individual. At the end of the activity, ask students to write a generalization about the values of their classmate based on the information they have recorded on the sheet.

Evaluation

Assess each activity individually as a class participation grade for cooperation and completeness. The paragraph writing can be evaluated as a formal writing assignment using a rubric.

Variation(s)

For handout 14F, ask students to bring a particular kind of object to class, such as a hat, something from their childhood, a favorite book, a special keepsake, or a favorite music CD. Based on the objects in a particular category, ask students to make inferences about each person's values and interests.

14A. MAKING INFERENCES BASED ON OBJECTS

Name: _____

(1 of 2)

1. Write 2 sentences describing the type of person who have these animals and objects in his or her house.

_____

_____

_____

2. List 6 objects that would be found in your bedroom that represent the type of person you are.

_____   _____

_____   _____

_____   _____

3. Write 2 sentences describing the type of person you are based on the 6 items just listed.

_____

_____

_____

_____

4. Choose 6 items that the character _____ or the real person _____ would own or that would best display the personality of this individual. Explain your choices.

_____   _____

_____   _____

_____   _____

Explanation:

_____

_____

_____

_____

5. Find one picture that represents you and explain its significance.

```



```

(2 of 2)

14B. USING VISUALS ON HOBBIES TO PRACTICE INFERENCE

Name: _____

Visual Hobbies

Directions: Using the clipart pictures, make some inferences and draw conclusions about the type of person each individual is based on the interests, hobbies, and possessions shown in the pictures.

Person 1

1. In what kinds of activities is this person involved? _____

_____

_____

2. What inferences can be made about the *kind* of person this individual is? What are the clues?

_____

_____

_____

3. Write 3 adjectives that describe this person.

_____

_____

_____

From *Reading and Writing to Learn: Strategies across the Curriculum* by Katherine Kuta. Westport, CT: Teacher Ideas Press. Copyright © 2008.

Name: _____

Behavior Traits

(1 of 2)

1. Describe the kind of father this person is based on pictures on the first page of the handout. Write at least 3 sentences and explain your inferences.

_____

_____

_____

_____

_____

_____

_____

_____

_____

_____

_____

2. Describe 5 qualities that this individual possesses, based on the pictures on the first page of the handout.

_____

_____

_____

_____

_____

_____

_____

_____

_____

_____

_____

_____

_____

(2 of 2)

From *Reading and Writing to Learn: Strategies across the Curriculum* by Katherine Kuta. Westport, CT: Teacher Ideas Press. Copyright © 2008.

14D. INFERENCES BASED ON SIGNS

Name: _____

Sign A	Sign B	Sign C

Sign D	Sign E	Sign F

1. What is the implied meaning of each sign? Explain your answers.

A. _____

_____

B. _____

_____

C. _____

_____

D. _____

_____

E. _____

_____

F. _____

_____

_____

2. How do the shapes add meaning to the signs? Explain.

_____

_____

(1 of 2)

3. What happens when there is a breakdown in the communication of the signs and symbols in society?

_____

_____

4. What are the 8 basic shapes of signs studied in drivers' education?

8-sided sign

3-sided sign

Round

Rectangle

Diamond

Pentagon (5-sided)

Orange square

Orange

Yellow triangle **Yellow**

5. Try to list at least 5 other universal symbols and write what each represents.

Example: = musical notes

6. Why is this nonverbal communication important in society?

_____

_____

14E. USING CLIPART TO MAKE INFERENCES ABOUT YOURSELF

Name: _____

Directions: Find 6 different pictures from clipart collections that best represent YOU. Cut and paste the pictures into the boxes below. Use the back of this sheet to prewrite your ideas, then write a paragraph explaining your choices on a separate piece of paper. Make sure you have a topic sentence that is a generalization, specific detail sentences, and a summary sentence at the end.

14F. MAKING INFERENCES BASED ON CLASSMATES' OBJECTS

Name: _____

Directions: We make educated guesses and draw conclusions about people every day. After each class member tells us about the visual object each person brought to share, record the person's name and picture and write an inference about that person.

Examples:

Person 1, grandmother's watch: Person 1 cares for his or her grandmother and values her watch.

Person 2, Chicago Cubs' hat: Person 2 is interested in baseball and the Cubs team.

Name of Person and Object	*One-Sentence Inference*

Activity 15

Monitoring One's Own Comprehension

Purpose of the Activity

The purpose of this activity is to give students the opportunity to practice the deeper level structure of comprehension called "monitoring" or "metacognition." Students become aware of what they know and do not know while they are reading. Active reading slows students down to interact with the text by reading for new ideas, deciding what they know or do not know, and asking questions about the text.

How to Use the Activity

This activity is a "during reading" activity, so students may interact with and comment on the text as they read. Use the strategy of "thinking aloud" to model the ideas of reading aloud and tell the class what you are thinking while the words are being processed inside your mind. Assign students a portion of the text and ask them to practice in pairs and share. At the independent stage, ask students to cut out the boxes on the handout and use the main ideas to group notes. Each person should take a turn sharing the notes and pasting them on a larger sheet of poster paper. These ideas can then be sorted into categories for further understanding.

As students share the information that is not understood and the questions, direct the discussion toward the specific misconceptions, questions, and interests of the class. The more authentic the interaction with text, the more ownership and comprehension will increase.

Evaluation

This activity may be counted as a class activity or a homework activity.

Variation(s)

Instead of using the activity handout, have students use three different colored Post-its® for each category and ask them to place them in the textbook at the points where they find interesting ideas, information not understood, and questions.

15. MONITORING COMPREHENSION

Name _____

Interacting with Text While Reading

Directions: First, cut out the 9 comment markers below. While reading pages
_____, fill in the 9 comment markers and place them between the pages of the
reading as bookmarks. Make sure you have support for why you put them where you did.

+ **Important Idea** **Why?**	**+** **Important Idea** **Why?**	**+** **Important Idea** **Why?**
– **Not Understood**	**–** **Not Understood**	**–** **Not Understood**
? **Questions**	**?** **Questions**	**?** **Questions**

From *Reading and Writing to Learn: Strategies across the Curriculum* by Katherine Kuta. Westport, CT:
Teacher Ideas Press. Copyright © 2008.

Activity 16

Connecting to Text:
Cooperative PowerPoint Review

Purpose of the Activity

The purpose of this activity is to offer students the opportunity to synthesize information by creating presentation slides on themes; symbols; quotations; connections to self, text, and the world; and main ideas to share with the class. Students become the teachers of the review of information from the content of the class and get the opportunity to learn from one another and take notes from the presentations.

How to Use the Activity

This post-reading activity requires the use of PowerPoint™ with the entire class. Time needed for preparation in a computer lab is about one week, and the time allotted for presentations will depend on class numbers. Allow students five minutes for their presentations, with a one minute grace period before and after the presentation before they will be penalized. Learning to fit projects within specified time allotments is an important skill. Have students work together so that while one is presenting, the other is working the computer and changing the slides. Have students sign up for specific days, scheduling eight (leaving room for absences) per day to give students a choice of when to present and the responsibility of being prepared.

Model an example of the presentation format by using previous student presentations or preparing one of your own. Don't forget to review the basic skills of using PowerPoint.

Students should synthesize the concepts from specific units by summarizing, presenting main ideas, and connecting the ideas in a specific format. This project is very engaging for students because there is a great deal of freedom and choice involved. The directions for each of the 10 to 12 slides are very specific, which forces students to read them carefully. The term *themes* refers to universal messages in literature. An example is, "If one sets goals for oneself, then one increases the potential of being successful." In social studies, science, or business, the term refers to the universal concepts that you want students to understand, such as the meaning of democracy or nationalism in social studies, photosynthesis and respiration or particular laws of science, or the law of supply and demand in business. Students must condense the specific ideas to state the "larger concept" for their classmates to hear one more time to reinforce the learning.

In locating a quotation of significance, students refer to the text and find specific support, practicing inference skills to explain the meaning, as well as giving credit to the writer.

Because comprehension involves connecting "old" with "new" knowledge, when students are searching for the three types of connections—self, other text, and the world—they are using their prior knowledge and research skills to locate specific examples to display in their presentations. For self, students could refer to life experiences at home, school, or work. For text examples, students could refer to a story, book, magazine article, movie, billboard, commercial, or other reading source. For world connections, students often like to use Internet sites about current events, newspaper links, or journal articles. A mini-lesson on URLs may be necessary. When reviewing or teaching hyperlinks, it is very important to discuss the need to locate and use legitimate sites and to identify the author of the site to check for credibility and authenticity. Students should know that domains ending in .edu, .mil, and .gov are reputable sites to reference.

Students must learn how to end a presentation with a summary instead of saying, "the end." A clincher statement is a phrase or sentence that sums up and closes the presentation as well as offering the audience something to think about in the future. Students need assistance and a mini-lesson on this topic not only for this presentation but also when they are writing formal papers.

Evaluation

Because this is a formal project, use a rubric featuring the points listed on the handout. Students have a tendency to put too much information on slides and do not consider the use of color, font size, placement of pictures, and proofreading. This project allows for mini-lessons about all the visual forms of communication. Another important area of communication is speaking skills, and students should be reminded to practice with their partners as well as timing themselves. This skill may become part of the rubric.

Variation(s)

To engage the audience, require the class to take three-column notes. Ask students to record the speaker's name, one concept presented that is worth remembering, and one picture memory cue. Have students use these notes to study for a future test. To increase motivation, the students could use the notes to write a letter to their teacher at the end of the semester explaining their own thoughts on their own learning. (See activity 60.)

16. CONNECTING TO TEXT FOR INCREASED COMPREHENSION

Cooperative PowerPoint Presentation (5 minutes Each Person)

Final Project: "Pulling It All Together" and Sharing with Others

Name: _____

Partner's Name: _____

Directions: As a review, you and your partner will be given separate unit topics to present to the class. Each person is responsible for his or her own presentation; however, you may help each other with preparation. Each person will be graded separately.

Topic/Unit 1: _____

Topic/Unit 2: _____

Partner Work Time: _____

Rough Draft Due: _____

Presentation Day: _____

Requirements: (These are the points of the rubric.)

1. Be prepared and on time

2. Provide colorful, creative, and original slides—include visuals

3. Include the significant content information

4. Provide accurate information and explain each slide

5. Follow the format and directions of the assignment

6. Speak loudly, slowly, and clearly

7. Use eye contact; do not read notes or constantly turn to read the screen

   - Each person is responsible for his or her own unit presentation following the format directions below.

   - Both people need to practice their presentations before delivery to the class.

   - Use key words and phrases on the slides with the visuals.

   - Do not try to put all the information on the slides.

(1 of 2)

From *Reading and Writing to Learn: Strategies across the Curriculum* by Katherine Kuta. Westport, CT: Teacher Ideas Press. Copyright © 2008.

Format:

Slide 1:   Title of project, your name, class, date, and period

Slide 2:   (1) State the unit title and include a symbol or picture to represent it. (2) State a 1-sentence theme or concept of the unit. (Explain the meaning orally. Do not use the word *you*.)

Slide 3:   State the title of the work, chapter, or article; author; and a quote from the text that is important to you. (Explain the meaning of the quote orally.)

Slide 4:   State 3 different types of connections. 1 = self, 1 = other text outside of the class, and 1 = the world.

Slides 5:   A, B, C: Show examples such as clipart, hyperlinks to pertinent Internet sites, or scanned-in photos to support your connections. (Explain each orally.)

Slide 6:   (1) State the next unit title and provide a symbol or picture to represent it. (2) State a 1-sentence theme or concept of the unit. (Explain the meaning orally. Do not use *you*.)

Slide 7:   State the title of the work, chapter, or article; author; and a quote from the text that is important to you. (Explain the meaning of the quote orally.)

Slide 8:   State 3 different types of connections. 1 = self, 1 = other text outside of the class, and 1 = the world.

Slides 9:   A, B, C: Show examples such as clipart, hyperlinks to pertinent Internet sites, or scanned in photos to support your connections. (Explain each orally.)

Slide 10:   End and sum up with a clincher slide.

From *Reading and Writing to Learn: Strategies across the Curriculum* by Katherine Kuta. Westport, CT: Teacher Ideas Press. Copyright © 2008.

Activity 17

Using Metaphor to Increase Comprehension

Purpose of the Activity

The purpose of this activity is to reinforce a concept through metaphor. Using metaphors increases learning by connecting new knowledge to concrete background knowledge to increase comprehension. Students will practice this figure of speech in both words and pictures about a content concept.

How to Use the Activity

Teach a mini-lesson on similes and metaphors. Similes compare two unlike things using the words *like* or *as*. Metaphors make a comparison by using a word for one thing in place of another to suggest a likeness between them. Explain that writers use these figures of speech to add meaning for the reader by using concrete comparisons for abstract words. Use the handout to model metaphor using the example of Pandora's Box. Explain that often allusions—literary, mythological, or biblical references—are used in readings. Use an abridged version of the Pandora story if background information is needed. Model another metaphor by creating one with a concept from the unit of study. For guided practice, assign concepts to pairs of students and have them create their own metaphors in words and pictures.

Evaluation

Students may be evaluated for their class participation, working in pairs on original metaphors, and sharing their products.

Variation(s)

Ask students to create metaphors for the key concepts at the end of a unit on a large piece of paper for class review, and post the papers on the walls for class viewing after they share.

17. WRITING TO LEARN: USING METAPHOR

Using Metaphor to Increase Comprehension

Pandora's Box: allusion (reference and comparison)

What is the reference in mythology? _____
Example: "This decision is Pandora 's Box."

Who is Pandora?

What is the reference to the Greek mythological woman being made?

This (think of an example) _____ is Pandora 's Box.

Explain the meaning of the metaphor comparison to the above picture:

Directions: Create a metaphor in words and pictures for the concept word assigned to you. Be ready to share your ideas with the class.

Concept: _____

Words: _____ is _____

_____

Picture metaphor: _____

_____

From *Reading and Writing to Learn: Strategies across the Curriculum* by Katherine Kuta. Westport, CT: Teacher Ideas Press. Copyright © 2008.

Activity 18

Creating Metaphors for the Deeper Meaning Structures of Comprehension, or "What Good Readers Do!"

Purpose of the Activity

The purpose of this activity is to help students create metaphors for deeper understanding of the skills that good readers use. According to Marzano (2004) and Sousa (2006), learning is increased through the use of metaphors because learners create comparisons between the abstract new knowledge and the concrete background knowledge and make new connections. Once the students understand the deeper meaning structures (using handout 18A), they can practice the skills whenever they read. In handout 18B, students must use higher level thinking skills to synthesize the habits of good readers and explain the concepts in both words and pictures for content concepts. In handout 18C, students extend this concept to their content understanding by creating a comparison of the content concept with their background knowledge and eight comprehension habits. In handout 18D, students use metacognition to monitor their own understanding of the comprehension skills and content for the lesson or unit.

How to Use the Activity

The students may use handout 18A to take notes on the comprehension structures while the skills are taught in mini-lessons or as practice with the content material. Handout 18A may also be assigned to be completed cooperatively or individually. If the activity is planned for the classroom, give students access to color markers or colored pencils to accommodate visual learners. Model this as a class before students are asked to work in guided practice pairs or independently.

With handouts 18A, B, and C, for students to learn from one another, use the cooperative strategy called "numbered heads." Assign a numbered box or term to each student; when their numbers are called, students with that particular number will stand up and share their work. Ask students to vote on which metaphor for each term or concept is the most effective as a memory cue.

With handout 18B, if these skills are being used with particular content, first have the students write the key ideas in the box and then create metaphors for the content in the circle to help them remember more effectively.

Students may also be asked to process and synthesize the information by evaluating which skill area they need to work on, by noting it on the back of handout 18B. Either give these concept terms directly to the students or allow them to choose their own. Review terms to reinforce the content lesson or unit. To complete the circle in handout 18B, ask students to work in pairs or individually to create metaphors The circle represents fitting all pieces together to create a whole. Ask students to use poster paper for the circle and to share metaphors aloud for additional reinforcement.

Have students use handout 18D as a post-reading activity for a content lesson, at the end of class period; as a homework assignment; as a think, pair, share activity with a partner; or as a review before a quiz. As students complete this activity, they must think about, reflect on, and take ownership of their own learning.

Evaluation

This activity may be counted as a class activity, homework activity, or quiz. Emphasize the process of creating the metaphor and explaining it to peers.

Variation(s)

One variation is to have students put the information on large poster paper so the it can be displayed in the classroom to emphasize either the terms (handout 18A) or the content metaphors (handouts 18C and 18D).

For kinesthetic learners, use concrete objects for the metaphors, such as plastic building blocks, wooden blocks, figurines, Styrofoam® pieces, or other small objects. For auditory learners, comparison to parts of music would be helpful.

18A. SYNTHESIZING: CREATING METAPHORS FOR COMPREHENSION

Directions: Write each of the "deeper structures" of comprehension listed below on a separate sheet of paper and explain it in terms of a metaphor, in both words and pictures. Each pair or group will share theirs with the class.

Previewing is . . .
In words:

In picture(s):

Connecting is . . .
In words:

In picture(s):

Visualizing is . . .
In words:

In picture(s):

Inferencing is . . .
In words:

In picture(s):

Finding Main Ideas is . . .
In words:

In picture(s):

Asking Questions is . . .
In words:

In picture(s):

Monitoring your own understanding is . . .
In words:

In picture(s):

Synthesizing is . . .
In words:

In picture(s):

18B. SYNTHESIS OF CONTENT

Name: _____

Directions: In the box below, define the concepts of the lesson or unit in your own words. In the circle, match the corresponding numbers with each wedge of the pie and think of comparisons (metaphors) to other things that are similar to the concepts, then complete the major concept.

Title of Unit and Pages: _____

Key Ideas/Terms to Know	
1.	5.
2.	6.
3.	7.
4.	8.

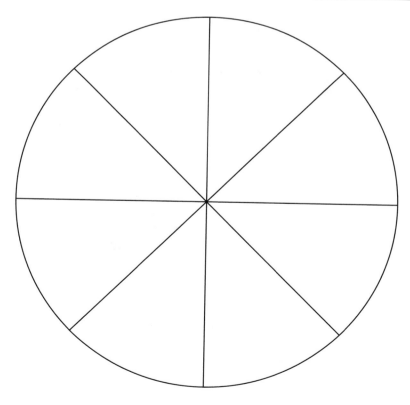

18C. SYNTHESIZING CONTENT NOTES

Directions: As you read your assigned material, use the 8 comprehension habits listed below and record your learning in the appropriate boxes. You may use words and pictures.

Title of Reading Material: _____

Name: _____

What Good Readers Do! Notes

Use vocabulary strategies	Visualize
Make inferences	**Ask questions**
Make connections	**Look for main ideas**
Monitor their understanding	**Synthesize the information** **Look for main ideas**

18D. USING COMPREHENSION STRATEGIES
TO REFLECT ON WORDS

Name: _____

Directions: Complete the following statements in complete sentences based on the content and your learning.

Making connections: This concept or reading reminds me of . . .	**Asking questions:** A "why" or "how" question is . . .
Stating the main point The most important idea to remember is . . .	**Creating a visual** A picture that I see in my head to help me understand this is . . .
Making inferences A conclusion or inference that I can think of today is . . .	**Monitoring your understanding** What do I not understand completely is . . .
Using Strategies to Learn A strategy that I used to increase my understanding is . . . And it improved my learning because . . .	**Synthesizing and Applying the Information to Myself** I can apply this information by . . . I can put the ideas together to remember this in 6 months . . . .

Activity 19

Fluency: Rapid Retrieval Strategy

Purpose of the Activity

There are three purposes for this oral reading comprehension activity. First, students use the text to practice scanning to answer the questions. Second, students read aloud to practice oral fluency. Third, students review the content material to reinforce main ideas and concepts that they are learning.

How to Use the Activity

This activity is probably best used as a post-reading exercise for review and scanning for information. Write the statements from handout 19B on the computer and project them on a screen or write them on an overhead projector transparency so that all students can easily see them. Share the directions and rules, and disclose the statements one at a time (handout 19B). This might be good to use as a game or as an opportunity for students to gain extra credit. Handout 19A offers a summation of a journal article, and handout 19B may be completed and used as an example. Both contain statement openers to use when writing content statements.

To increase motivation and success, direct students to work in pairs, asking both students to raise their hands when they have the answer. If the activity is used as a game, students will compete to be first to raise their hands. Have them state the correct page number and read the exact words of the answer aloud . Keep track of their points on white eraser boards or by passing out some kind of chip, card, or paper. After the completion of the exercise, students may count their points and record them.

Evaluation

This activity may be assessed for class participation points and/or extra credit points.

Variation(s)

Ask students to process three ideas that they did not understand before the activity and that they now need to remember or study. These notes may be written in their notebooks or turned in as "exit slips," which are papers or index cards that students turn in as they exit the classroom, usually for credit. These "exit slips" help the teacher identify items for further reinforcement or review.

Comprehension and Fluency

("Rapid Retrieval of Information: Reading Aloud with a Purpose." *Journal of Adolescent & Adult Literacy* 41:4 (December 1997/January 1998))

Rapid retrieval of information focuses on the strategy of oral re-reading:

- to answer a question

- to prove a point

- to provide an example from the text after silent reading

- as an alternative to answering the end of chapter questions

Skills involved:

- Higher-level thinking skills to decide what information needs to be retrieved
- Critical thinking strategies such as drawing inferences, evaluating, and analyzing
- Knowledge of synonyms and parts of speech
- Scanning for specific information
- Skimming to find the words or paragraphs to complete the task
- Active listening to the part being read
- Use of the authentic text in the classroom
- Repetition of key ideas for comprehension

Suggested Openers:

- Read aloud the sentence that states . . .
- Find proof that . . .
- Read aloud any paragraphs that support the idea of . . .
- Find a phrase of . . . words from the text to be substituted for the word . . .
- Read aloud a section of the text that you feel gives the overall summary of the whole text.

Other Suggested Strategies to Practice Fluency:

- Repeated readings
- Paired readings

19B. RAPID RETRIEVAL OF INFORMATION FOR INCREASING FLUENCY AND COMPREHENSION

Directions: Only one1 numbered item will be displayed at a time. The goal for you and your partner is to find the exact words in the textbook that correctly explain what is asked for, and then both raise your hands first to be called on to give the correct page number and read aloud the requested information. If correct, you get _____ points.

Topic: _____

Chapter: _____ **Pages:** _____

1. Read aloud the sentence that states
_____

_____

2. Find proof that _____

_____

3. Read aloud any paragraphs that support the idea of _____

_____

4. Find a phrase of _____ words from the text that can be substituted for the word

_____

5. Read aloud a section of the text that you feel gives the overall summary of the whole text

_____

_____

6. Read the caption to the illustration that displays _____

_____

7. Read aloud the definition of the word _____

8. Find the most important concept in the chapter and read the 2–3 sentences that best explain it._____

_____

_____

_____

9. Read an important idea that you think will be on the test. _____

_____

10. Find the explanation of the problem or process stated in this unit for _____

_____

_____

Activity 20

Practicing Fluency with Children's Books

Purpose of the Activity

Because fluency is necessary for comprehension, this activity provides oral reading practice for students, who work in pairs and read aloud to one another. Oral fluency is a skill that should only be used for assessment or for performance, not for comprehension of difficult text. By using easy children's books, which contain the elements of fiction, students can easily connect to the content being studied, or they can perform for a younger audience. Students interact with words, pictures, the story elements, and each other. Students from a very early age through high school are expected to know and understand the elements of "prose fiction," as it is called on the ACT reading test. Most state reading tests require this basic understanding of literary terms, and this activity provides reinforcement. This activity presents students with the idea of previewing many books and making choices based on their observations, so they can practice and learn not to choose a book "just by the cover."

Handout 20A is especially useful for students who are second language learners, because they will be more successful with fluency using easy reading books, as well as becoming more familiar with American culture and increasing background knowledge.

Handout 20B offers students guided practice with the elements of fiction through the reading of easy stories.

How to Use the Activity

Visit the school or public library to give students access to a wide collection of children's materials. State the purpose of the activity at the beginning. Tell students that the purpose is to read to practice identifying the elements of fiction, to read children's books that relate to a particular unit of study, or to practice fluency for a younger audience. Once they understand the purpose, older students are motivated to preview and read the children's books.

It is advisable to model fluency and to do a think-aloud with the entire class so that students can listen and hear the difference between reading to an audience and reading for oneself. Also during the think-aloud, ask the students to take notes on the elements of fiction to review them. If the think-aloud is making a connection to content concepts, model this also. Another skill to model is how to preview and how to choose a book. Readers often look at the front and back covers, illustrations, the topic, the author, and the visual appeal. Students need to open the book and read a couple of pages to see if the book catches their interest.

Choice also improves motivation, so handout 20A asks students to choose three books to read silently first for practice with silent fluency. Then the students will share their reading with a peer to practice reading aloud for an audience. Students are asked to process the areas of fluency, such as following punctuation, using intonation in their voices, reading slowly, and sounding natural and effortless. Students can discuss this with their partners. Then students must evaluate which book they liked, make a connection to their content, and complete handout 20B. Students should realize that all fiction stories have many of the same elements.

Evaluation

There are several areas to assess, such as participation in the fluency exercise, cooperation with a partner, and completion of the written portion of the activity.

Variation(s)

Arrangements could be made for students to read to younger students in the school district, to preschool classes in the same school building, or to younger classes in other schools in the community. One opportunity that lends itself to this activity is Dr. Seuss's Day, "Read Across America." Students especially enjoy reading to younger children; affectively the older students feel more positive about reading, and the younger children get to see the older students as models of readers.

20A. READING TO LEARN: PRACTICING FLUENCY WITH CHILDREN'S BOOKS

Previewing:

Do you have a favorite memory from your childhood of a book that was read to you? What do you remember? _____

_____

_____

Find 3 titles of books that look interesting and record the titles and authors here.

1. _____

_____

2. _____

_____

3. _____

_____

What factors helped you choose these books? _____

_____

_____

Practice reading each book 3 times, with a different partner each time. Make sure you read loudly, slowly, and clearly. Take the time to show the pictures, make predictions, and talk about the theme of the book.

1. Partner _____ Book _____
2. Partner _____ Book _____
3. Partner _____ Book _____

Write 3 suggestions for improvement for reading to smaller children.

1. _____
2. _____
3. _____

Which book did you like best, and why?

_____

Is there a connection that you can find between a concept or theme in the book and a lesson or unit that you are studying in a class? Explain. _____

_____

_____

_____

From Reading and Writing to Learn: Strategies across the Curriculum by Katherine Kuta. Westport, CT: Teacher Ideas Press. Copyright © 2008.

20B. USING CHILDREN'S BOOKS FOR CRITICAL THINKING

Directions: All fiction books at every level have similar elements. Complete this organizer on each of the children's books.

Title of Book and Author	Title of Book and Author	Title of Book and Author
Plot (State in 1 sentence) Conflict	Plot (State in 1 sentence) Conflict	Plot (State in 1 sentence) Conflict
Main character: 3 adjectives for each	Main character: 3 adjectives for each	Main character: 3 adjectives for each
Setting (where and when)	Setting (where and when)	Setting (where and when)
Mood (How did the story make you feel?)	Mood (How did the story make you feel?)	Mood (How did the story make you feel?)
Theme (What was the message of the story, in 1 sentence?)	Theme (What was the message of the story, in 1 sentence?)	Theme (What was the message of the story, in 1 sentence?)
Connection (Is there a connection to yourself, text from class, and/or the world?)	Connection (Is there a connection to yourself, text from class, and/or the world?)	Connection (Is there a connection to yourself, text from class, and/or the world?)
Other elements: irony, foreshadowing, symbolism, tone	Other elements: irony, foreshadowing, symbolism, tone	Other elements: irony, foreshadowing, symbolism, tone

Part 2

Reading and Writing to Learn, Involving Affective and Cooperative Learning

Activity 21

Cooperative Learning: Appointment Clock

Purpose of the Activity

The purpose of the appointment clock is to create multiple opportunities for students to read, write, and talk together in pairs. The appointments allow students to meet a variety of people in the class.

How to Use the Activity

The appointment clock can have as many numbers on it as the teacher desires. It can be used for a class period, an entire school day, a week, or longer. At the beginning of the class, explain that there is only one appointment for each of the numbers used on the clock. If six appointments are being requested, ask for three boys and three girls, or six people who do not sit near each other, to be clock "buddies." Give students a couple of minutes to fill in their clocks with appointments. Then, when you are ready to complete a "Think, Pair, Share," or another cooperative activity, call out the number of the appointment that the students must find to complete the task. If students do not have an appointment for the requested number on the clock, then they must come to the front of the room to be paired up or put in a group of three if necessary.

The appointment clock can be used with many of the other activities in this book that involve guided practice, pairing, and cooperative grouping.

Evaluation

This activity is used as a tool to enhance cooperation and discussion in the classroom, so the task involving the appointments may be either evaluated individually or counted as a participation grade.

Variation(s)

To get a variety of pairings or groups, a deck of playing cards, wrapped candy pieces, a miniature matching objects, clipart, photos, or famous quotations can be used to mix up the students when placing them in groups. Some preparation time is necessary. Sort and count the objects so that the number of pieces equals the number of students. There should be an identical number and kind of cards, objects, or candy for each pair or group, for example, two red kings form a pair or two chocolate candies form a pair. Pass out the playing cards at the door as the students enter the room. When the class begins, ask students to find the person who has the same card, object, or candy that they have. This random grouping is fun and gives students the opportunity to work with a variety of people in the class.

Students can also just pick the sorted candy pieces from a jar and form pairs or groups based on the choices that match.

21. COOPERATIVE LEARNING: APPOINTMENT CLOCK

Name: _____

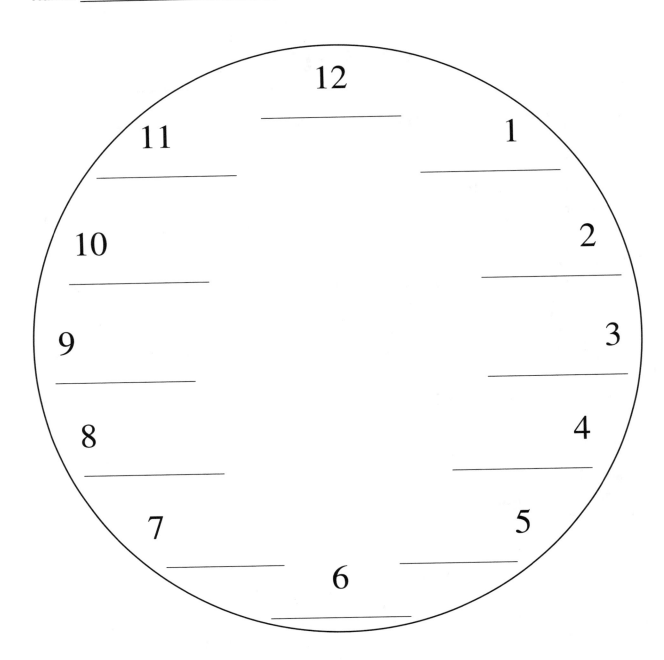

Activity 22

Affective Learning: Tombstone Test

Purpose of the Activity

The purpose of this activity is to have students evaluate their own goals and the affective domain. This writing exercise asks students to think, set goals, write, share their thoughts, and paraphrase another person's ideas. Students need to learn to work cooperatively with other people, and this exercise offers them an opportunity to connect with other members of the class. In the paired sharing and class discussion, some conclusions could be drawn from students' responses. Almost always, the responses will involve affective comments referring to emotions, feelings, and/or social connections. Since the affective needs of the student must be met first for learning to occur, this activity helps establish connections and a comfort level with peers.

How to Use the Activity

This activity could be used at the beginning of a new semester or new school year. It's safe for all students because it does not involve risk taking, all students can participate in and complete the activity unless they choose not to, and it is interesting for most students. Therefore, this activity is highly motivational. Ask students to think about the future and predict how they want to be remembered by their classmates. Explain to them that students often return many years after graduation for a class reunion and exchange memories of school with former classmates. In this activity students are asked to think about their values and impressions of people that often are lifelong memories. Ask students to do the writing in class and share and discuss their answers.

Evaluation

Assess this either as a class activity to emphasize the affective nature of learning or as a writing response assignment. If assessing as the , students may be given participation credit for completion. If assessing as the latter, a rubric should state the main points of emphasis for grading. Finally, offer students an additional point or two for practicing fluency, sharing, and responding to a classmate's writing.

Variation(s)

This activity can be adapted to fit a content lesson. Substitutions for the word *student* in the handout could be *friend*, *sibling*, or *classmate*. In a content class the phrase could be changed to "How do you think the character, historical person, scientist, or famous person, _____, would want to be remembered?" Depending on the audience, the word *students* could be replaced by *teachers*, *parents*, or *mentors*. Most of the time, the answers are affective in nature.

22. AFFECTIVE LEARNING: TOMBSTONE TEST

Directions: Complete the following sentence and explain your answer in several sentences. Then find a partner to share responses with. Summarize your partner's response in one sentence below.

I WANT TO BE REMEMBERED AS A STUDENT WHO . . .

_____

_____

_____

_____

_____

_____

Name of Partner: _____

Explain in your own words your partner's response: _____

_____

_____

_____

Activity 23

People Search: Preview or Review

Purpose of the Activity

There are several purposes for this activity. By using the affective people search (activities 23A and 23B), students will have an opportunity to get to know one another through one-on-one conversation as well as a chance to connect with one another by sharing a specific detail or experience. The content search (activity 23B) may be used as a preview exercise to pull out background knowledge or as a review exercise to allow students to "walk and talk" about the content material and display ownership of learning. Students also process the information that is still unclear and unknown by labeling their focus for future study. Finally, activity 23C may be used to teach the difference between a "generalization" and a "specific detail," using the people or content search information.

How to Use the Activity

After the handout for activity 23A is distributed and directions are clearly stated to the class, students can be timed while mingling and talking to one another about the items on the sheet. By taking notes about their classmates and writing down their names, students will remember their classmates' names and feel more comfortable working with others cooperatively. After the allotted time is up, use the handout for activity 23C to have the students practice the concept of "generalization vs. detail." Students sometimes have problems writing a focus/thesis statement for their essays and research papers and choosing strong supporting details for the focus, and they can practice this important concept using the "people search." One question to ask students is, "What similarities do all of you have in common that could be stated as one general statement about the people in this class, based on the data produced by the search?" Then ask students to share individually so those who may not understand completely can listen to other students' sentences as models. The next step is to ask students to write a sentence, using the same data, containing a specific detail to support their statements.. Once again, ask students to share their responses with the class.

In activity 23B, the content search, students play an active role in the preview or review of the key vocabulary terms and/or unit's concepts by "walking and talking" about the content material with their peers. In planning for using this activity, the terms and concepts may be filled in the boxes on the handout and duplicated for the class. Students will then search for the definitions and explanations as well as get names of students who share, to prove who talked to whom during the interview process and learn their classmates' names. At the end, students may be asked to highlight the boxes containing the information that they are least familiar with so that they know that they must read and study these topics again. If there are boxes that cannot filled in by anyone, then the class needs more guided practice in those areas. After discussion, the sheet can be used as a study guide for a quiz or test at a later date.

Evaluation

This activity could be counted as a class activity, or students may be given additional points for finishing the activity first, second, and third.

Variation(s)

Students may take more ownership of the activity if groups are assigned lessons or units to work on together to create their "content search" for the specific chapter or material assigned. Then the most pertinent boxes could be combined for the end of the quarter or semester review.

23A. STUDENT PEOPLE SEARCH: "GET TO KNOW YOUR CLASSMATES"

Directions: This activity allows you to "walk and talk" to your classmates as you search for people who match one of the "people search" questions. Make sure you record each person's answer and his or her first name.

Name of Student: _____

1. Find a person who has been in another state.

State _____ **Person's name** _____

2. Find a person who has read a novel within the last month.

Novel title _____ **Person's name** _____

3. Find a person who has eaten carrots in the last month.

Name of vegetable _____ **Person's name** _____

4. Find a person who likes to play card games.

Name of game _____ **Person's name** _____

5. Find a person who has broken a bone.

Bone _____ **Person's name** _____

6. Find a person who likes to hike.

Where? _____ **Person's name** _____

7. Find a person who has seen a movie in the last week.

Movie title _____ **Person's name** _____

8. Find a person who has a career goal.

Goal _____ **Person's name** _____

9. Find a person who has more than 3 siblings.

How many? _____ **Person's name** _____

10. Find a person who likes to cook.

Favorite dish _____ **Person's name** _____

11. Find a person who plays 2 sports.

Sports _____ **Person's name** _____

12. Find a person who likes ice cream cones.

Favorite flavor _____ **Person's name** _____

13. Find a person who has read a magazine in the last week.

Magazine title _____ **Person's name** _____

14. Find a person who has met a celebrity.

Celebrity _____ Person's name _____

15. Find a person who plays an instrument.

Instrument _____ Person's name _____

16. Find a person who has seen a play.

Play title _____ Person's name _____

17. Find a person who likes to dance.

Kind of dance _____ Person's name _____

18. Find a person who has a pet .

Type _____ Person's name _____

19. Find a person who likes the color green.

Why? _____ Person's name _____

20. Find a person who plays a guitar.

For how long? _____ Person's name _____

21. Find a person who rides a skateboard.

Where? _____ Person's name _____

22. Find a person who likes to shop.

Where? _____ Person's name _____

23. Find a person who has climbed a tree.

Where? _____ Person's name _____

24. Find a person who likes to read graphic novels.

Novel title _____ Person's name _____

25. Find a person who knows how many students attend the school.

How many? _____ Person's name _____

26. Find a person who can say, "Hi, my name is ____. It is great to meet you" in another language.

Language _____ Person's name _____

27. Find a person who does not like pizza.

Why not? _____ Person's name _____

28. Find a person who has eaten a mango.

Where? _____ Person's name _____

(2 of 2)

23B. STUDENT CONTENT PEOPLE SEARCH

Name: _____

Directions: Find a student who can define the term or explain the concept, record his or her answer, and write down his or her first name. Sit down when you finish, then highlight or circle the 5 main concepts that you need to study and remember for the future.

Chapter or Unit: _____ **Pages:** _____

1. Find a person who can define the term _____	1. Find a person who can explain _____
2. Define here: _____ _____ _____	2. Explain here: _____ _____ _____
3. Classmate's name _____	3. Classmate's name: _____
1. Find a person who can define the term _____	1. Find a person who can explain _____
2. Define here: _____ _____ _____	2. Explain here: _____ _____ _____
3. Classmate's name _____	3. Classmate's name: _____
1. Find a person who can define the term _____	1. Find a person who can explain _____
2. Define here: _____ _____ _____	2. Explain here: _____ _____ _____
3. Classmate's name _____	3. Classmate's name: _____
1. Find a person who can define the term _____	1. Find a person who can explain _____
2. Define here: _____ _____ _____	2. Explain here: _____ _____ _____
3. Classmate's name _____	3. Classmate's name: _____
1. Find a person who can define the term _____	1. Find a person who can explain _____
2. Define here: _____ _____ _____	2. Explain here: _____ _____ _____
3. Classmate's name _____	3. Classmate's name: _____

(1 of 2)

From *Reading and Writing to Learn: Strategies across the Curriculum* by Katherine Kuta. Westport, CT: Teacher Ideas Press. Copyright © 2008.

1. Find a person who can define the term _____	1. Find a person who can explain _____
2. Define here: _____ _____ _____	2. Explain here: _____ _____ _____
3. Classmate's name _____	3. Classmate's name: _____
1. Find a person who can define the term _____	1. Find a person who can explain _____
2. Define here: _____ _____ _____	2. Explain here: _____ _____ _____
3. Classmate's name _____	3. Classmate's name: _____
1. Find a person who can define the term _____	1. Find a person who can explain _____
2. Define here: _____ _____ _____	2. Explain here: _____ _____ _____
3. Classmate's name _____	3. Classmate's name: _____
1. Find a person who can define the term _____	1. Find a person who can explain _____
2. Define here: _____ _____ _____	2. Explain here: _____ _____ _____
3. Classmate's name _____	3. Classmate's name: _____
1. Find a person who can define the term _____	1. Find a person who can explain _____
2. Define here: _____ _____ _____	2. Explain here: _____ _____ _____
3. Classmate's name _____	3. Classmate's name: _____
1. Find a person who can define the term _____	1. Find a person who can explain _____
2. Define here: _____ _____ _____	2. Explain here: _____ _____ _____
3. Classmate's name _____	3. Classmate's name: _____

(2 of 2)

23C. GENERALIZATION VS. DETAIL

Name: _____

Generalization

- A broad, abstract statement
- General and oversimplified
- A universal statement
- Arguable
- A summation
- An opinion

Detail

- A fact
- A specific feature
- Provable
- A piece of information
- Unarguable
- Concrete

Directions: Write a one-sentence generalization based on the information from the people or the content search. Then write one sentence that contains a specific detail supporting the general statement.

Generalization: _____

_____

_____

Specific Detail: _____

_____

_____

What did you learn from this activity, and how can this relate to writing an essay or research paper?

_____

_____

_____

_____

From *Reading and Writing to Learn: Strategies across the Curriculum* by Katherine Kuta. Westport, CT: Teacher Ideas Press. Copyright © 2008.

Activity 24

Share an Idea and Get an Idea

Purpose of the Activity

The purpose of activity 24A is to engage students by asking them to preview their prior knowledge about reading and writing.

Activities 24B and 24C are intended to engage students with text in a content area. This activity requires students to critically choose information to share, summarize their ideas, write the main ideas succinctly, read their peers' comments, choose interesting ideas, and share main ideas that are worth repeating. Students are participating in several learning style modes. Visual learners connect to the Post-its® and posters, and auditory learners connect to the oral sharing of the ideas. In addition, since there is movement around the classroom, kinesthetic learners are actively engaged in walking from poster to poster to place and remove Post-its.

How to Use the Activity

Activity 24A, can be used at the beginning of the year. It is designed to preview background knowledge about what "good readers do," and to preview successful study skills. Activity 24B is designed to be used with content material and is designed for five separate sections of content material. The handout can be duplicated for more sections of text. Use Activity 24C to help students process key concepts and key vocabulary terms.

Some preparation is necessary for these activities. They require four large pieces of poster paper to be taped on the wall in separate areas of the room, with each labeled with one of the titles being discussed. If there are four titles, then each student would need to have –four or five Post-its for the activity. The participants first write three to five ideas on the handout, then must choose one in each category to write on a Post-it or on large poster paper, as directed in class. For accountability, students should also write their first names at the bottom of each Post-it in case questions come up. After all students have written their comments on Post-its, they should be directed to move around the classroom and place the appropriate Post-it on the matching large poster paper.

After all the Post-its have been placed on the poster paper, ask the students to walk around the room and read the various comments. Direct them to find two NEW or INTERESTING comments that are not their own and then return to their seats. After everyone is seated, have students read aloud their chosen Post-its for each main idea, concept, and vocabulary word.

The activity 24C handout may be used to help students take notes on the main ideas of their peers. Ask the students to take notes on the content material shared in class. By condensing their key ideas to one page, students' comprehension and ownership are increased.

Evaluation

This classroom activity can be assessed in terms of participation, cooperation, and completion of the notes. Often simply offering students the chance to get an "A" or "zero" for the task is a strong motivation for interest and participation.

Variation(s)

The activity could be used as a unit review. Assign students different sections of the text that they have previously read and ask them to focus on the key ideas of each section and place those on the posters with Post-it notes. Then have the students walk around the room to read the posters and record the key ideas that they do not remember and need to study for the test. Different colors of Post-its could be used to distinguish between various groups of texts.

24A. COOPERATIVE AND AFFECTIVE LEARNING: SHARE AN IDEA AND GET AN IDEA

Name: _____

Previewing Background Knowledge

Directions: Answer the following questions. Then choose the one response that is worth repeating and sharing with others. Using 4 Post-its and write one idea on each from each response. Be sure to initial each Post-it. Afterward, place each Post-it on the large paper on the wall. Each person will read the ideas and choose 2 ideas that others have written, to share aloud.

1. What are 3 ideas, strategies, or facts that are important to share about "reading"?

_____

_____

_____

2. What are 3 ideas, strategies, or facts that are important to share about "writing"?

_____

_____

_____

3. What do "good readers" do to understand what they read?

_____

_____

_____

4. What kinds of reading and writing do students need to do, to learn and to pass their classes?

_____

_____

_____

> During the oral discussion, write down at least one interesting NEW idea that was shared!
>
> _____
>
> _____
>
> _____

From *Reading and Writing to Learn: Strategies across the Curriculum* by Katherine Kuta. Westport, CT: Teacher Ideas Press. Copyright © 2008.

24B. COOPERATIVE AND AFFECTIVE LEARNING: SHARE AN IDEA AND GET AN IDEA USING NOTES

Directions:

- Use this sheet as a guide to for thinking and to record important main ideas from your notes that are worth repeating.

- **Choose** one main idea from each category and **record** it on a Post-it. Put your name or initials on each one.

- Then **share** your Post-its by placing them on the large posters that are labeled with the sections or chapters being studied. Circle or highlight your main idea choices on this handout.

- **As directed, walk around the room and** choose from the posters on the wall 3 Post-its from other classmates that you think contain important ideas to share aloud in class.

Fill in the Chapter Title: _____ ,

Pages: _____

1. From Section _____, pages _____, write down the 5 most important **vocabulary concepts** and **important key ideas** that are needed to understand the reading.

_____
_____
_____

2. From Section _____, pages _____, write down the 5 most important **vocabulary and key ideas** that are needed to understand the reading.

_____
_____
_____

3. From Section _____, pages _____, write down the 5 most important **vocabulary concepts and key ideas** that are needed to understand the reading.

_____
_____
_____

4. From Section _____, pages _____, write down the 5 most **important vocabulary and key ideas** that are needed to understand the reading.

_____
_____
_____

5. From Section _____, pages _____, write down the 5 most **important vocabulary and key ideas** that are needed to understand the reading

_____
_____
_____

From *Reading and Writing to Learn: Strategies across the Curriculum* by Katherine Kuta. Westport, CT: Teacher Ideas Press. Copyright © 2008.

24C. RECORD OF IDEAS FROM STUDENT SHARING

Processing Information

Directions: For each section being reviewed in class, record at least 1 vocabulary concept and 1 key idea that you need to study for the test.

Section _____, Topic _____

Vocabulary Concept _____

Key Idea _____

_____

Section _____, Topic _____

Vocabulary Concept _____

Key Idea _____

_____

Section _____, Topic _____

Vocabulary Concept _____

Key Idea _____

_____

Section _____, Topic _____

Vocabulary Concept _____

Key Idea _____

_____

Section _____, Topic _____

Vocabulary Concept _____

Key Idea _____

_____

Section _____, Topic _____

Vocabulary Concept _____

Key Idea _____

_____

Activity 25

Affective Reading and Writing Survey

Purpose of the Activity

The purpose of this activity is to ask students to tell how they feel about reading and writing. By asking them to evaluate how they view these skills at the beginning of a school year or semester, and then again at the end of school year or semester, any change in outlook in either of these learning processes can be seen, including any major shifts in attitude and learning. Students are being asked to monitor and think about their own learning.

How to Use the Activity

At the beginning of a course, ask students to answer questions on the handout in complete sentences. Explain to them that the purpose of the activity is to find out their feelings and point of view about reading, writing, and learning, which will be based on past experiences. Tell them that outlook, views, and attitude can be changed through positive learning experiences both in and outside of school. By sharing the goal of wanting all students in the class to be both readers and writers by the end of the course or school year, the teacher gives students a better understanding of your point of view. At the end of the course or school year, students can repeat the survey and compare their responses, which may or may not have changed over time. Follow this with a class discussion or written response.

Evaluation

This survey may be assigned class participation points, and the handout may placed in students' individual portfolios. Since there are both pre- and post- surveys, the number of student changes in affective attitude could be used for reports at the end of the year.

Variation(s)

This activity certainly could be modified to assess students' feelings and attitudes about any content area. Sometimes students have bias based on insufficient information about or experiences with specific topics or subject areas. By asking students to write out and discuss these feelings up front, you will generate more student awareness, and students will take more ownership in their learning, both affectively and cognitively.

25. AFFECTIVE READING AND WRITING SURVEY

Name: _____

Directions: Answer the following questions.

I am a reader, or I am not a reader. Why or why not?

_____
_____
_____
_____
_____
_____

I am a writer, or I am not a writer. Why or why not?

_____
_____
_____
_____
_____
_____

I like the subject matter _____ or I do not like

the subject matter_____

Why or why not?

_____
_____
_____
_____
_____
_____

Activity 26

Parent–Child Questionnaire

Purpose of the Activity

This activity is designed to involve parents in their children's education as well as have students practice authentic notetaking. Each student must record his or her answers to the questions in class, and then for homework or at a parent open house or conference night, the student must record the parent's responses. The activity is also designed to open up communication between parent and child about the student's grades, study habits, and growth as an individual. Students also use authentic writing to find specific information and record it.

How to Use the Activity

Because the questions are personal and self-explanatory, the activity could be done either in class or as homework. As an assignment, require students to administer the questionnaire to one or both parents and share their personal responses with their parents. The students should count and record the number of parent answers that were correct and ask the parent(s) to sign the form at the bottom. The next day the class may discuss or write about which questions and answers most surprised the parents and about the need for communication in families.

Evaluation

This activity could be graded as a class activity or serve as a springboard to a writing response activity in which the students make connections to their world and relationships. Another possibility is having the students write down their responses to, "Why should parents know their children?" or "Is it important to have positive relationships in a family?"

Variation(s)

Students could be asked to write a questionnaire for siblings or friends and then repeat the process of this activity. A discussion should take place in the classroom about the kinds of questions that should and should not be asked on questionnaires and surveys.

26. PARENT–CHILD QUESTIONNAIRE

Name of Student: _____

How Well Do You Know Your Child? Questionnaire

Question	Parent Responses	Child Responses
1. What makes your child really angry?		
2. Who is your child's best friend?		
3. Who is your child's hero or her-oine?		
4. What embarrasses your child most?		
5. What is your child's greatest fear?		
6. For dessert, would your child prefer a milkshake, a cookie, a piece of fruit, or a candy bar?		
7. What is your child's favorite subject?		
8. What is the subject your child dislikes the most?		
9. What is your child's favorite color?		
10. Where does your child like to sit in the classroom?		

(1 of 2)

Name of Student: _____

How Well Do You Know Your Child? Questionnaire

11. What is your child's favorite book?										
12. About which accomplishment does your child feel the proudest?										
13. What gift from you does your child cherish the most?										
14. What person outside the family has influenced your child's life the most?										
15. What is your child's greatest complaint about the family?										
16. What did your child eat for lunch one day this week?										
17. What is one idea, concept, word, or fact that your child learned this week?										
18. What is one study habit that your child needs to improve?										
19. How many of your answers do you think will match your child's answers?										
20. How many of his/her answers do you think your child predicted that you will match?										

Activity 27

Writing: "Positive Feel Good" Messages

Purpose of the Activity

One of the purposes of this activity is for students to relate to each other in a positive manner by writing positive statements to one another. Since research has shown that our emotions and feelings control our ability to focus and learn, it is very important for students to feel comfortable expressing themselves in the classroom and to connect to one another individually so that they can work cooperatively as a team. Also, students will practice their writing skills by expressing themselves in authentic, meaningful statements.

How to Use the Activity

This activity can be used near the beginning of a school year or new semester to encourage students to talk to get to know one another. However, it may be used whenever it seems appropriate. A connection to a content area could be made, for example, with the young adult novel *Ironman*, by Chris Crutcher. At one point in the book, the anger management teacher has the students write "positive comment Valentine messages" to one another. This activity would be a good fit with the novel.

To preview, students may have a discussion about the purpose of sending holiday greeting cards. After passing out the handout, explaining the directions, and stating the purpose of the activity, model several comments for other teachers or students, such as "I appreciated the time you helped me with passing out papers"; "Thank you for being my think, pair, share partner"; or You seem like a very organized person." Give students time to walk around and talk to each other to check on names and their spelling. Ask students to write in the boxes on the handout a certain number of comments or one for every member of the class. They should sign the comment slips. The comments may be collected and read first to check for appropriateness, or, if the teacher is comfortable with the climate of the classroom, the slips can be cut up and passed out without being reviewed. Students should then read the comments and process the activity by thinking about and reflecting on the task. One question to ask students is how they felt while reading the positive comments from their peers. Students may be asked to express either orally or in writing how thinking and feeling positive is necessary to be healthy in everyday living.

Evaluation

This activity can be assessed as a class activity for participation, a writing activity, or extra credit points.

Variation(s)

A connection with this activity is to bring in other texts that deal with "positive thinking." The best seller *The Secret*, by Rhonda Byrne, could be assigned for more reading on this topic, as well as various self-help books. For extra help students could look for titles or more information on "positive attitudes," "the history of Valentine's Day," "the history of greeting cards," or "writing for greeting card companies."

For another authentic writing experience, ask students to write a "thank-you" note to someone at the school who has helped them .

27. WRITING: POSITIVE MESSAGES

Writing "Positive Feel Good" Messages

Name: _____

Directions: After filling in one class member's name in each box, think of something positive to write about that person that will bring a smile to his or her face. Then sign your own name. The teacher will cut the boxes into slips and distribute them. Think of these comments as friendship "Valentines," because everyone here is part of a team.

To:

From:

To:

From:

To:

From:

To:

From:

To:

From:

To:

From:

Activity 28

Cooperative Learning Using Jigsaw and Notetaking

Purpose of the Activity

The purpose of the cooperative learning activity is for students to read nonfiction, informational text and take notes, which will develop their ownership in and expertise about an assigned topic. Students will then be able to share important ideas with classmates and learn how to practice actively reading for main ideas and specific supporting details by employing a concise notetaking method. They will also listen listen to their peers and summarize the information gathered in order to teach it to their classmates. Comprehension increases when students teach something to others.

How to Use the Activity

This activity can be used with a textbook, journal articles, or other informational readings. Before doing this "jigsaw" cooperative activity (handout 28A), model and practice the skills of notetaking and finding main ideas with supporting details. Some additional advance planning is needed to divide the reading piece into sections. Depending on the length, three to four readers per piece is suggested to maintain continuity of the reading. Each group of four may read the same material, or each group may have its own section to read and share with the class. The material should be divided up as evenly as possible. If the text has boldface headings, use those as breaking points. Divide students into groups by having them draw colored cards from a box, with each color designating a different group. Give students directions and tell them the amount of time they have to read and take notes.

After each student has completed the task of notetaking, beginning with Reader 1, have each take a turns sharing his or her notes with the other students in the group. Each member should make notes based on classmates' main ideas using the activity 28B handout.

If all the groups used the same sections, have a class discussion about that material. If important items were missed, students may be given a chance to add to their notes in a different color ink, to make them more complete. If each group was assigned different sections of the text, then all students need to take careful notes on the parts that were not assigned to their own group. One suggestion is to hand out an overhead transparency to each group so that the group's notes would become visual, for the visual learners. If a projector is available, the students' notes could be projected from the handouts or the students' notebooks.

Evaluation

Students should receive credit for participating in the activity and be evaluated on how well they took and recorded notes. Remember that students need to practice a skill, strategy, or cooperative activity several times before they achieve a comfort level and ownership. Ask students to evaluate the notetaking in a cooperative group setting in terms of their own learning and understanding of the material. Students are quite honest in their assessments, and processing a task is also part of having students "write to learn."

Variation(s)

If all groups of students are assigned the same text, then another step can be added. To engage students even more, especially kinesthetic learners, after they take their individual notes for each part assigned, ask them to find three other people who were assigned the same reader number. For example, the Reader 1s would form a group; the Reader 2s would form a group, and so forth. Each person may take a turn sharing his or her information, while the others check their own notes for accuracy and completeness. Then the 1s, 2s, 3s, and 4s would think of a visual way to teach the others the information learned in the original groupings. The students would share the information through both words and picture memory cues.

28A. JIGSAW NOTE SHEET

Name: _____

Reading Material: _____

Section and pages: _____

Directions: Take notes in words, then try to condense the notes into a couple of key concepts, and then draw illustrations of the concepts as memory cues to teach others.

Notes
Key Concepts
Picture Form of Notes

Notes from Group Members

Key Words for Section (Use your own words)	**Notes on Main Ideas** (Use your own words)
Reader 1	
Reader 2	
Reader 3	
Reader 4	

Activity 29

Cooperative Learning: Information Poster

Purpose of the Activity

In this activity students actively read for specific purposes, as directed on handout 29, and to write concise, succinct notes to help them teach others. Students work together to produce an attractive poster with precise, compelling information to use as an aid to their learning. They practice their oral communication skills. The specific reading skills, such as main ideas, important supporting details, making connections and inferences, visualization, purposeful reading, and vocabulary, are all included on the poster. Several learning styles (visual, auditory, and kinesthetic) are involved in this activity; the best practices—using cooperative learning, using nonlinguistic representations for information, having students teachg students, summarizing, and practicing metacognition strategies—are all involved in this activity.

How to Use the Activity

This activity involves some advance planning. As always, the teacher should model the steps before assigning the activity to students. The teacher must divide up the text that will be used. Because this is a jigsaw, meaning that each group is a part of the complete puzzle, each group assumes responsibility for part of the reading. It is best to assign students to groups of three or four, because there are three bullets in many of the boxes on the poster. Students could each be assigned a specific color marker in order to ensure accountability for each response. Assign students a specific section to read and take notes. Then each group member shares the information and records important ideas on the notetaking sheet. The members then decide together what information would be best to put on the poster. Finally, the groups share the information with the class and the class members are asked to take notes in their notebooks and/or walk around the room and take notes from the hanging posters. When students are asked to share and teach others, learning and remembering are increased. This activity allows for ownership of both teaching and learning.

The box that asks students to think about the "strategies" that were used for understanding is part of the "monitoring" or "metacognition" strategy employed by all good readers. These are the "fix-up" strategies that good readers use to increase their understanding. It is helpful for all students to listen to their peers share strategies such as re-reading, underlining, notetaking, actively highlighting, asking questions, and talking about the text.

Evaluation

This activity may be evaluated in a number of ways. Students may be given credit for actively reading and notetaking, as well as participation points for working with team members. The students may also be asked to rate themselves and the group cooperation on a scale of 1 to 10 and to discuss ways to improve performance in completing the task in a group setting. Finally, the presentation and poster may each be scored with a rubric for a formal grade on the content.

Variation(s)

This activity would also work well with a variety of articles or other readings, with each group teaching an article or reading to classmates. Groups could use the two-colum notetaking system (see activity 41A handout) to record notes for their presentations of content material. The poster requirements could be altered to focus on other skills or more content, such as illustrations, graphs, and/or features of the text.

29. COOPERATIVE LEARNING: INFORMATION POSTER

Name: _____

Jigsaw Presentation on Poster Paper

Author/Title: _____

Source and Date of Text: _____

Group Members: _____

Remember each bullet point is a contribution by each team member!

Major Concepts	Purpose of the Text
• _____	• _____
• _____	• _____
• _____	• _____
• _____	• _____
Important Facts	**Connections to Text (Self, Text, World)**
• _____	• _____
• _____	• _____
• _____	• _____
• _____	• _____
Inferences	**Important Vocabulary (Max 3)**
• _____	• _____
• _____	• _____
• _____	• _____
• _____	• _____
What strategies did you use for understanding?	**Visual Image for Remembering a Concept**
• _____	
• _____	
• _____	
• _____	

Write large, use colored markers, decide on how and what information wil be shared, and prepare to teach the information cooperatively to the class. Everyone must participate and everyone must share. All will take notes on each presentation.

From *Reading and Writing to Learn: Strategies across the Curriculum* by Katherine Kuta. Westport, CT: Teacher Ideas Press. Copyright © 2008.

Activity 30

Reading Critically for Understanding

Purpose of the Activity

The overall purpose of this activity to give students repeated practice with deeper meaning comprehension skills, so that eventually students will actively read in content areas by finding main ideas, observing illustrations, making connections, asking questions, processing, and reflecting on the information. By recording and discussing their findings, students will also learn from one another.

How to Use the Activity

This activity handout can accompany an article, textbook reading, or other nonfiction piece of any size. The students should be familiar with the terminology of the six questions, and the activity should be modeled with an entire class to ensure they understand what to do. If the students need more guidance, the desired number of key ideas could be stated at the onset. After students are familiar with the questions, they may work in groups for guided practice before working independently. After completing the activity students will monitor and comment on their own understanding to see if it has increased. Ask students to reflect on and evaluate a specific area for to focus on in future.

Evaluation

This activity could be evaluated as a whole group class activity, a paired class activity, or an individual assignment. Since part of the activity is objective (factual) and part is subjective (opinion), students may assess their own handouts and add other students' comments to them in another color during the general discussion.

Variation(s)

The parts of the text chapter, book, or article, may be "jigsawed," and each pair or group would be responsible for only a section of the reading. Students would take notes on the other sections.

30. READING CRITICALLY

Name: _____

Reading to Learn: Improving Understanding

Topic: _____ **Reading Pages:** _____

Author: _____ **Source:** _____

Key Ideas: (Usually 1 main idea per paragraph.) Look for repetition or dark print words in the text

_____

_____

_____

Illustrations: List the pictures, diagrams, charts, and graphs used to focus on the main ideas, and explain the purpose of each. _____

_____

_____

_____

Connections: Choose 1 or more of the 3 kinds of connections to the reading.

Self: (personal experience) _____

_____

Text: (book, film, billboard, song, magazine, or other kinds of visual images)

_____

World: (connection to something in society) _____

_____

Questions: _____

_____

_____

Reflect: What have I learned from this reading that I want to share with others, and remember 6 months from now? _____

_____

_____

Fact vs. Opinion: Write down 1 fact and 1 opinion from the reading.

Fact: _____

Opinion: _____

From *Reading and Writing to Learn: Strategies across the Curriculum* by Katherine Kuta. Westport, CT: Teacher Ideas Press. Copyright © 2008.

Activity 31

Connecting to Poetry

Purpose of the Activity

The purpose of this activity is for students to connect poetry to themselves or the concepts in the content material that they are studying. Using poetry to practice connections, inferences, and implicit themes improves understanding of the structures of comprehension. Students also practice using figures of speech and fluency as they read their poems to other students. They also gain an appreciation of the genre of poetry.

How to Use the Activity

Because choice improves motivation, give students the choice of finding using a poem that has meaning to them from either a book or the Internet. Schedule time in a library or resource area for a librarian to review how to look for poetry in various sources. Assign content concepts, time periods, feelings, or cultures to help them focus their search. Review poetry terms and model the activity in class before students work on this activity independently. The terms that need review are boldfaced on handout 31 to focus attention on them.

To improve fluency, students should read their poems to two people, who may be class members or adults, A few minutes a day can be devoted to students reading their poems aloud for class members to enjoy and discuss. If time is limited, ask students to read and explain only their favorite line from the poem.

Evaluation

The assessment may be done of researching a poem, completing the activity sheet, reading the poem to others, and sharing in class.

Variation(s)

For more practice with visualization, the activity can include visuals that display the theme, mood, or symbolism of the poem. The poem should be typed and pictures placed around it that are related to it in a significant way. This visual representation could be added to the class sharing portion of the activity.

31. FINDING A POEM TO CONNECT TO SELF, TEXT IN CLASS, OR THE WORLD

Directions: Using the poetry books in the library, the Internet, or your own collection, find a poem that connects to you, a poem that connects to a concept from the readings in this class, or a poem that connects to a concept in the world. Complete this analysis, copy or type out the poem, cite the source correctly, practice reading the poem aloud several times, get signatures from 2 people, and prepare to share the poem and the information with the class.

Name of Poem (in quotes): _____

Poet: _____

Source: _____

Type of Connection (self, text, world). Explain: _____

_____

Analysis

1. Number of lines in poem: _____

2. Number of **stanzas**: _____

3. Type of form or structure of poem: (**free verse, cinquain, ballad, sonnet,** etc.)

_____

4. Find a figure of speech and/or poetic device in the poem, such as a **simile, metaphor, personification, hyperbole, alliteration,** or **onomatopoeia** and explain the meaning. Write the exact line(s), in quotes:

_____

Explain the meaning: _____

_____

5. Write an example of **imagery** that displays the senses (sight, sound, taste, smell, and/or feel) and explain the meaning of the descriptive words. Write the exact line(s), in quotes:

_____

Explain the meaning: _____

_____

6. Write the meaning of the poem in one sentence: _____

_____

7. Write how the poem makes you feel: _____

_____

8. Write why you chose this poem to read to the class: _____

_____

9. Read your poem aloud to two people and have them sign their names to show that they heard it:

1) _____

2) _____

10. Write your favorite line from the poem: _____

_____

From *Reading and Writing to Learn: Strategies across the Curriculum* by Katherine Kuta. Westport, CT: Teacher Ideas Press. Copyright © 2008.

Activity 32

Understanding Nonfiction Using a Magazine

Purpose of the Activity

The purpose of this activity is to have students practice the necessary skills that "good readers" perform automatically while they read as well as to practice the test taking skills that are needed for mandated testing. The use of magazine articles allows students to practice these skills using authentic nonfiction text. Since most students need to use a strategy or practice a skill a minimum of seven to ten times through direct instruction and guided practice before moving toward independent use, this activity provides an opportunity to focus on specific skills repeatedly. Students need to know the type of text they are reading, and how to read for a purpose, to think about the main ideas, to ask questions as they read, to figure out vocabulary in context, to consider the bias of the author, to paraphrase an author, to summarize an article, and to make connections to what is read. Model this activity with the class and then use it again as guided practice before asking students to use it independently.

How to Use the Activity

Use this activity as a teaching tool employing *Newsweek, Time for Kids, Time*, or other current events periodicals. A good authentic text to consider for practice is the "My Turn" essays that are published in *Newsweek*. First, explain to students the differences among narrative, expository, and persuasive essays. They also need to understand that the type of essay depends on the text structure that the author used to develop the focus or ./thesis. Transitional words are signals used by the writer to connect ideas for the reader and to create a structure within the piece of writing. Teach students that an essay is subjective and a news story is objective. The understanding of each type of articles should be modeled by the teacher.

Since all nonfiction articles, especially news stories, are based on the 5 "Ws"—who, what, when, where, and why (is this important), as well as how (does this relate to me)—teach students to ask these questions as they read . Students should automatically ask these questions as they read text passages.

In addition, if the text is an essay, teach students to read for the main idea, focus, or thesis. In the "My Turn" essays, for example, the focus is always stated beneath the title of the article. For news articles, the focus is a combination of the 5 Ws in one sentence. Make sure students are given examples of good writing to read; this modeling is necessary for them to become good writers themselves.

Two important writing skills to teach are paraphrasing and summarizing. Many students do not understand the difference between these skills, yet they are used for writing research papers and reports. Paraphrasing is replacing the author's words with one's own words (not necessarily the same number of words). Summarizing is condensing the number of words into a shorter version containing the same meaning and including the beginning, middle, and end. The shorter the summary, the more difficult it is to write, because more details must be eliminated.

The most difficult skill for students to acquire is identifying the tone and bias of the author. The *tone* is the author's style or way of expressing himself or herself in the writing, and the *bias* is the author's attitude toward or preconceived idea about (or prejudice toward) the subject matter. Because identifying tone or bias is an inference based on text clues, this skill is difficult and should be practiced often. Both state tests and the ACT reading test ask questions about the TONE of the reading. To model this for students, point out who the author is and his or her background. Then, during active, careful reading, students should circle the words revealing emotion. Finally, these clues should be discussed to reach an educated guess about the tone and implied bias of the author. The *mood* is the reader's feeling toward the topic, character, or the writing.

In terms of understanding vocabulary, students may be asked to select their own words, or words may be pointed out during previewing of the text. Students should be asked to use three to five words to complete the vocabulary map in the handout, and they should then choose one word to teach the class. Ask class members to record the vocabulary words in their notebooks, including other requested information (part of speech, definition, and a visual memory cue). These notes can be arranged in column form for easy reference.

Evaluation

This activity may be evaluated for completeness, as a class or homework activity, or for oral sharing of information. Depending on the skill focus and time available, ask students to share an interesting article, an example of bias by an author, a new vocabulary word, a fact, or an opinion of an authority quoted for support in an article.

Variation(s)

Ask students to record notes about each other's sharing, in pairs or as a whole class. Ask various students to teach one word from handout 32 to the class and have the class record the new vocabulary in their notebooks for future reference.

32. UNDERSTANDING A MAGAZINE ARTICLE

Name: _____

Title of Magazine: _____

Date of Magazine: _____

Choose an article that is at least 1 page long.

Title of Article: _____

Author: _____

Pages of article: _____

1. What type of nonfiction text is this article: expository or persuasive (circle one)? Explain how you know the type of writing being used. _____
_____

2. As you read, answer the 5Ws to gather information.
   - WHO or WHAT IS the article ABOUT?
   - WHAT IS IMPORTANT?
   - WHERE?
   - WHEN?
   - WHY IS THIS IMPORTANT?
   - HOW DOES THIS RELATE TO ME?

3. Write down the focus or main idea, in 1 sentence. _____
_____
_____

4. Write a 5-sentence summary using the 5Ws information; include the main idea and 3 important factual details. _____
_____
_____
_____
_____

5. Choose a sentence from the article and copy it. (Page _____.)Then paraphrase it in your own words to capture the same meaning as the original text. (Remember your sentence should be nearly the same length.) _____
_____
_____

(1 of 2)

Your paraphrase: _____

_____

_____

6. What is the tone or bias of the author? Explain, and give 1 or 2 examples of emotional words from the text that support your answer. _____

_____

_____

7. Write 1 or 2 sentences about something you learned or found interesting that you would like to share with the class. _____

_____

_____

_____

_____

8. Find 1 vocabulary word to share with the class. Complete the following vocabulary map.

DEFINITION in   **CONTEXT SYNONYM**

_____   _____

VOCABULARY MAP

Part of Speech

Original sentence from the magazine, in quotes, and page number

_____

_____

_____

YOUR OWN ORIGINAL SENTENCE   **SYMBOLIC PICTURE**

_____

_____

_____

9. Record the new vocabulary words taught by your classmates.

_____

_____

_____

10. What strategy is most helpful to you to enable you to understand nonfiction material, and why?

_____

_____

_____

(2 of 2)

Activity 33

Bookmark of Information

Purpose of the Activity

In this activity students are asked to create a useful tool that can be used as a compact study aid. They are required to condense textual information into succinct main ideas and important ideas and list the information in a small amount of space. Also, they must state the overall concept in one sentence, create picture memory cues, and write definitions for significant vocabulary from the selected reading. In completing a bookmark, students are interacting with the text, finding main ideas, visualizing, focusing on vocabulary, and synthesizing information.

How to Use the Activity

Show students various bookmarks and discuss the p uses of bookmarks: for marking a place in the reading, for marketing new materials, and for communicating specific information in a small amount of space. Ask students to take two-column notes while they read in pairs or independently. Then give them the activity 33 handout, copied on heavier paper, and have them cut out the bookmark. Use a different color for each chapter. Students may then share and use their their bookmarks to study.

Evaluation

Assess this activity as a class activity or homework assignment. Students can share the bookmarks in class and display them on a bulletin board.

Variation(s)

One variation of this activity is to jigsaw the parts of the reading (see activity 29) and ask pairs or individuals to create a bookmark for a particular paragraph, section, article, story, or chapter. Then the pairs or individuals could share the information as a teaching or review activity. If there are several different selections of text, the bookmarks could be passed around for peers to read.

If the amount or kinds of information need to be changed, ask students to create their own bookmarks. If displaying the bookmarks on the walls or a bulletin board, enlarge the handout so that they will be easier to read.

33. CREATING AN INFORMATIONAL BOOKMARK

Name: _____

Bookmark the Information!

Title of Reading Material: _____

Topic: _____ **Pages:** _____

Directions: Using the template below, create a bookmark on paper to help you condense the main ideas of the reading and create memory cues for increased comprehension. Use the back of the bookmark as directed or to record notes.

Bookmark

Topic: _____

Pages: _____

Main Ideas (fewer than 8 words each)

_____

_____

_____

_____

_____

Major concept of reading in 1 sentence:

_____

_____

_____

_____

_____

Memory cue for concept:

_____

_____

_____

_____

_____

New vocabulary:

_____

_____

_____

_____

_____

_____

From *Reading and Writing to Learn: Strategies across the Curriculum* by Katherine Kuta. Westport, CT: Teacher Ideas Press. Copyright © 2008.

Activity 34

Using *Newsweek* Magazine for Reading and Writing

Purpose of the Activity

The major purposes of this activity is to have students read current nonfiction and practice the comprehension skills of reading for main ideas and details; making connections to self, text, and the world; understanding the difference between fact and opinion; making inferences; and monitoring their understanding. Students need to practice these skills repeatedly until they become automatic while they are reading independently. Both state tests and the ACT nonfiction reading passages ask comprehension questions that require using these skills

How to Use the Activity

Model the comprehension areas listed when introducing the magazine. It does not matter if various issues are used in the classroom. *Newsweek* contains a variety of information, and the table of contents should be previewed with the students. Some students may not be familiar with the structure of the magazine. Explain that the "Periscopes" section is a series of short news updates that offer a small glimpse of the news, just as a periscope on a submarine offers a small view what is above the water. For question 2 in the handout, tell students to use articles at least one page long that focus on world, national, and local news, not features or human interest stories. Question 3 asks students to make observations about one advertisement. A mini-lesson about propaganda devices or the methods used by advertisers to appeal to their audience may be necessary. For question 4, refer students to the section called, "Newsmakers," or choose five other stories about individuals or places. In question 5, students are asked about their own learning and to write three sentences displaying ownership of their learning. For closure, ask students to share one of their sentences aloud in the classroom. This sharing can be accomplished rather quickly and offers all students a chance to practice oral fluency.

Evaluation

Assess this activity as a class or homework activity. Use handout 34 for a discussion on current events, examples of specific reading skills, or preparing for state testing.

Variation(s)

One option is to add a vocabulary activity such as the "Vocabulary Map" from this book (activity 32 handout). Students could be asked to find three vocabulary words that are new to them and then share one with the class. They could also be asked to record the new vocabulary in their notebooks.

Another suggestion, for practice for state and ACT writing tests, is to use the weekly, "My Turn," essay as a model of well-written essays. Sometimes the writers are teenagers, and students are particularly interested in reading text written and published by other young people. Each essay should be discussed in terms of focus, support and elaboration, organization, grammar mechanics, and the integration of all these factors to achieve one purpose.

34. READING AND WRITING USING *NEWSWEEK*

Newsweek **Issue:** _____

Name: _____

1. Read 3 "Periscopes" and write 1 main idea/fact that you learned from each.

A. Title: _____

Main Idea: _____

B. Title: _____

Main Idea: _____

C. Title: _____

Main Idea: _____

2. Read 1 article of interest that is at least one full page long. Look for an interesting idea, 3 facts, and 3 opinions.

Title and page: _____

One Interesting Idea _____

_____

Facts:_____

_____

_____

Opinions: _____

_____

_____

3. Choose an ad, cut it out, staple it together, and make an inference about it.

Ad: _____

Inference: _____

_____

4. People and places in this issue. Find 5 people and 5 different places in the news. Tell why each is there.

People   **Places**

_____   _____

_____   _____

_____   _____

_____   _____

_____   _____

5. Describe in 3 complete sentences 3 current events that you learned about today.

A. _____

_____

B. _____

_____

C. _____

_____

Activity 35

Reading and Writing: Comprehending
Reader's Digest Magazine

Purpose of the Activity

Many students lack background knowledge about everyday events. The purpose of this activity is to involve students in everyday reading for life using the monthly periodical *Reader's Digest*. The activity handout directs students to specific sections of the magazine and gives the students guided practice on reading and writing skills such as previewing, finding main ideas, working with vocabulary, practicing making inferences, summarizing, connecting to background knowledge, and synthesizing text. Students need to understand the following types of texts: table of contents," quotations, feature stories, medical objective news, and other informational kinds of text. There is also a focus on verbal skills, asking students to share new knowledge with the class. The ultimate goal is to have students use these skills independently when they read.

How to Use the Activity

Since many students may not be familiar with this periodical, a walk through of the sections of the magazine would be helpful. Modeling the questions and skills from the handout will help students understand the deeper meaning strategies that "good readers do" for increased comprehension as well as to read for a purpose. It is suggested that you give the page numbers of the particular sections so that students become familiar with the structure of the magazine. Then students could work together in pairs for guided practice and move toward independence. Another suggestion is to offer several choices of feature stories that seem more appropriate for students or related to content material. When students are given some choice," they tend to be more motivated to complete a task. After the activity has been completed, either in class or for homework, discuss the various sections as time permits.

Evaluation

This activity can be assessed as a class or homework activity. Parts can be changed or eliminated as needed.

Variation(s)

If only one copy of each monthly issue is available in the library, this handout can be used to accommodate using issues from a variety of months, since the format is very similar in every issue.

35. READING AND WRITING USING *READER'S DIGEST*

Name: _____

Date of Issue: _____

1. What are the main story and the picture on the cover? _____
_____

2. Page_____. Preview the table of contents and name 3 interesting articles or stories.
_____
_____

3. Page _____. Go to the "You Said It" section. This section is similar to "Letters to the Editor"; read 1 letter and state the reader's point in 1 sentence.
_____

4. Page _____. In the "Only in America" section, read 3 of the short articles and write down 3 interesting facts. _____
_____
_____

5. Page _____. In the "Everyday Heroes" section, read about 1 person and explain why that person is in the news as a hero. _____
_____

6. Page _____. In the "Word Power" section, write out the vocabulary words and take the challenge by matching definitions. Then correct it using the answer key on the next page in the magazine. Choose the 5 most difficult words and write a sentence and memory cue for each.

1.	11.
2.	12.
3.	13.
4.	14.
5.	15.
6.	16.
7.	17.
8.	18.
9.	19.
10.	20.

(1 of 3)

Words to Learn:

1. _____
2. _____
3. _____
4. _____
5. _____

7. Page _____. In the section, "Medical Update," read 2 articles and write what you learned. _____

_____

_____

8. Page _____. In the section, "Quotable Quotes,, choose 1 quote, write it down, state whether you agree or disagree, and connect to it in some way.

Quote: _____

_____

Author: _____

Response: _____

_____

9. Page _____. In the section, "Laughter, the Best Medicine," explain the implied message of the lines, or in other words, what makes it funny.

_____

_____

10. Page _____. In the section, "RD Living" state 4 facts.

1. _____
2. _____
3. _____
4. _____

11. In the "Features" section, here are the choices to read. **Only read 2 selections.**
Suggested readings:

_____

_____

_____

Reading No. 1—Title: _____

Page: _____ **Author:** _____

Summary: 5–7 sentences _____

_____

_____

_____

_____

_____

(2 of 3)

From *Reading and Writing to Learn: Strategies across the Curriculum* by Katherine Kuta. Westport, CT: Teacher Ideas Press. Copyright © 2008.

Opinion of the Piece: 3 sentences

_____
_____
_____
_____
_____
_____

Reading No. 2—Title: _____
Page: _____ **Author:** _____
Summary: 5–7 sentences

_____
_____
_____
_____
_____
_____
_____
_____
_____
_____

Opinion of the Piece: 3 sentences

_____
_____
_____
_____
_____
_____

12. What was your favorite reading or section of the magazine, and why?

_____
_____
_____

13. What would you like to share with the class on sharing day?

_____
_____
_____
_____

Activity 36

Literacy Circle: Reading for Information

Purpose of the Activity

There are several purposes for this cooperative learning activity. It is called "Literacy Circle" because this strategy focuses on understanding informational text. By taking on literacy roles and engaging in interactive, interdependent groups, students take ownership for their own learning as well as becoming "experts" on the topic. Another purpose is to have students share and take notes on a graphic organizer, in which one box represents each section of text (see below).

How to Use the Activity

This activity requires advance planning and organization. The text could be previewed, and students could be asked to take notes on the text and/or actively read the material as a class activity. Divide students into groups of four. Provide a different colored graphic organizer for each role. (The graphic organizer is a sheet on which eight boxes have been drawn.) In each group of four, have students randomly choose a particular role: notetaker, connector, illustrator, or questioner. Students should then join other students who have the same role to work together to complete their assignment. After a limited amount of time, students will return to their original groups to share their ownership of their roles and new information. Ask students to share one new idea "worth repeating" and to write a processing statement on the activity handout.

Evaluation

Students can be assessed for active reading, notetaking, learning a role, sharing, and working cooperatively. The entire activity can be counted as class participation points.

Variation(s)

For more information, to consider other roles, or to develop literature circles with fiction, consult works by Dr. Harvey Daniels, especially *Literature Circles: Voice and Choice in the Student-Centered Classroom* (Stenhouse 1994). This activity is an adaptation of his suggestions for nonfiction reading.

Literacy Circle

Name: _____

Text: _____

Author: _____

Day 1: Preview text and take notes while reading for main ideas in words.

Day 2: Jigsaw the roles (each person takes ownership for 1 role) to increase understanding of the text and then group sharing.

Roles:

1. Summarizer: Write 1 main idea in fewer than 8 words (8 total).

2. Connector of Ideas to Self, Text, World: Write 1 example of each per section (8 total).

3. Illustrator: Draw 1 picture for each main idea (8 total).

4. Questioner: Write 1 inference question per section (8 total).

Group Members' Names and Roles:

1.

2.

3.

4.

Directions:

- A different colored graphic organizer has been provided for each role. Since everyone has already read the material and has taken two-column notes, each person will meet with the other students who have the same colored sheet and the same role to complete the activity.

- All members of the new group should help each other complete the task assigned as well as discuss and share.

- Return to the original groups to take turns sharing your findings.

- During the last few minutes of class, each person will contribute 1 idea worth repeating, for all to hear.

Processing: How did this activity increase your understanding of the text and your learning?

_____

_____

Activity 37

What I Learned While Reading . . .

Purpose of the Activity

The purpose of this activity is have students read for background knowledge and general information. They learn that reading involves getting meaning from print. Students also practice writing in complete sentences.

How to Use the Activity

Use activity 37 as a previewing exercise for students to gain background on a topic by having them read research and articles from newspapers and/or magazines. By recording the new information, students become aware of new knowledge. Have students rank the information in order of importance or have them share the most important ideas about the topic. In *Reading Reasons: Motivational Mini-Lessons for Middle and High School,* Kelly Gallagher supports the idea that students need to read to improve reading and to learn.

Evaluation

Evaluate activity 37 as a class participation activity and as an exercise in writing complete sentences.

Variation(s)

Another option is to have students read a variety of background material and share the ideas they acquire with the class in activity 24, "Get an Idea and Share an Idea."

For pleasure reading of the newspaper, have students record new information about current events.

37. WHAT I LEARNED BY READING_____

Name: _____

Directions: After choosing material to read, make a list of the information that you learned in the time allowed that you did not know before.

Text and pages: _____

Minutes spent reading: _____

Source for material: _____

1. _____

2. _____

3. _____

4. _____

5. _____

6. _____

7. _____

8. _____

9. _____

10. _____

11. _____

12. _____

13. _____

14. _____

15. _____

Activity 38

Writing a Story Based on a Picture/Photograph

Purpose of the Activity

There are several purposes for this activity, which can be implemented in any content area. This writing exercise involves students with the comprehension skills of visualization, observation and inference, critical thinking, understanding the main ideas of the elements of fiction, predicting, and connecting the text with their writing. Since the students can be directed to photographs and drawings related to a particular content area or topic of study or to people connected with the subject matter, there is flexibility in the assignment

One purpose of this activity is to give students the opportunity to do creative writing based on a drawing or photo from the suggested museum sites. Students get to practice making visual observations and making inferences to plan a story. This activity also serves as a review of the major elements of fiction: plot, setting, character, mood, theme, and point of view. These literary terms are included in all state standards as well as being tested on the ACT.

Another skill covered by this activity is "fluency." Students have the chance to read their stories aloud to one another and share their ideas. By reading and sharing their stories aloud either in pairs, groups, or to the whole class, they are practicing fluency and improving their reading. Classmates will practice critical listening skills to check for point of view and record an interesting comment about the writing. Finally, students will learn that good writing involves using interesting vocabulary and varied word choices.

How to Use the Activity

Because choice is a strong motivating factor for students," you may allow students the freedom to choose their own pictures to write about. Or you may prefer to offer the students a just a few selections related to a specific theme or topic. It is advisable to model planning and writing a story with the entire class. It would also be helpful to review the literary terms before the assignment. The assignment is set up for three class periods, but can be adjusted.

This activity involves some previewing of the sites to find specific pictures. These sites should be bookmarked for students to refer to in a computer lab. If only one computer is available in the classroom, then one particular picture could be projected, and students could work in groups or pairs to write their stories.

This activity takes several class periods to complete. On the first day, one class period is needed for students to preview the site and find one picture that they like, connect to, or find interesting. The photo or drawing should be bookmarked, saved, or printed so that the students can easily find it again. Time is needed in class, study hall, or at home for the brainstorming of the elements of the story, which can be done using the activity sheet. Direct students to write a rough draft based on their notes and then revise it, possibly with a partner. This can be an in-class assignment or homework. Divide students into groups of three or four to form "Writers' Circles." Students each take a turn reading their drafts aloud, and the listeners complete the third step on the handout by commenting on the stories in writing. Tell students to listen for the elements of fiction, the theme of the story, the creativity of the writer, or a connection to the content material. Have students write two or three sentences about what they learn from this activity.

Evaluation

The steps of the process may be assessed, or a rubric could be used to check off the specific elements that are covered in the assignment. For example, if the purpose is for students to practice writing a creative story using the elements of fiction and to complete the writing process successfully, then the rubric checklist could include completion of brainstorming, rough drafting, inclusion of 5 story elements, individual revision, sharing with at least two others, listening and commenting to two peers, and processing the learning.

Variation(s)

If computers are unavailable, another option is to choose a book on photography, a book on art from a particular museum, or postcards of famous artworks. One such example is Ken Russell's photographs from the turn of the century depicting child labor, which could be used to accompany a unit in social studies on immigration, the 1900s, or child labor.

For more whole class involvement and practice of prediction and inference skills, pictures could be hung on a bulletin board or taped to the chalk edge at the front of the room. Then as students take turns reading their stories, they may discuss which picture matches the story and the reasons for their guesses. By discussing the reasons for their choices, the students are learning that inferences are educated guesses based on facts that support their opinions.

Another possibility is to work with the librarian to obtain appropriate visual materials.

38. USING A VISUAL TO CREATE AND WRITE A STORY

Directions: Find a photograph/drawing/painting you are interested in creating a fictional short story about. Assume a particular point of view and use your creativity to involve the visual information in the story. Some choices are to create a character based on the picture, use an object (symbol) from the picture, imagine a setting, or invent a conflict and plot.

Day 1, Part 1: _____ Preview the visuals at the following Web sites. Choose one, print it out, and brainstorm ideas for your creative story. You should use the plot triangle (below) and take notes.

Suggested sites:

- http://lcweb2.loc.gov/ammem/browse/ Library of Congress
- www.loc.gov//rr/print/guide/ Library of Congress: prints and photos
- www.metmusieum.org Metropolitan Museum of Art
- www.ameicanart.si.edu/index2.cfm Smithsonian Institution
- www.artic.edu Art Institute of Chicago

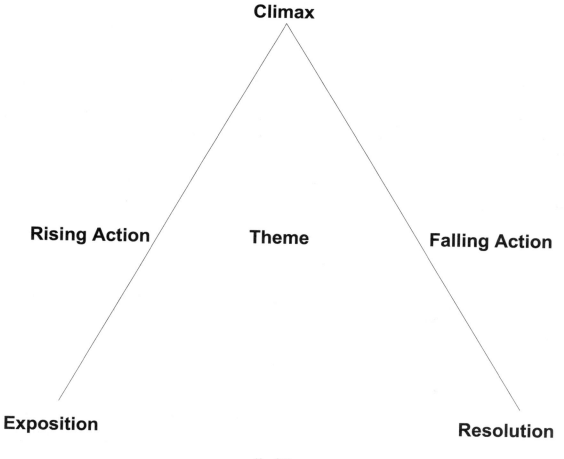

(1 of 2)

From *Reading and Writing to Learn: Strategies across the Curriculum* by Katherine Kuta. Westport, CT: Teacher Ideas Press. Copyright © 2008.

Day 2, Part 2: _____ Write the story in class and revise it. Remember to include the elements of fiction that all stories must contain

Elements of Fiction: Character, Plot, Setting, Mood, Theme, and Point of View (Optional: Irony, Foreshadowing, and Symbolism)

Day 3, Part 3: _____ Stories will be read aloud in class to encourage fluency. Each class member will write comments about the other readers' stories.

Reader: _____

Student Critic: _____

Interesting Comments: _____

_____

_____

Day 3, Part 3: _____ Stories will be read aloud in class to encourage fluency. Each class member will write comments about the other readers' stories.
Reader: _____

Student Critic: _____

Interesting Comments: _____

_____

_____

Day 3, Part 3: _____ Stories will be read aloud in class to encourage fluency. Each class member will write comments about the other readers' stories.
Reader: _____

Student Critic: _____

Interesting Comments: _____

_____

_____

Day 3, Part 3: _____ Stories will be read aloud in class to encourage fluency. Each class member will write comments about the other readers' stories.
Reader: _____

Student Critic: _____

Interesting Comments: _____

_____

_____

(2 of 2)

Activity 39

Using Music and Dance to Learn

Purpose of the Activity

There are several purposes for this activity. First, it allows students who are auditory and kinesthetic learners to excel via their learning style and display ownership for their learning. Second, since the brain is wired to respond to music to increase connections and learning, students have the opportunity to incorporate all their senses in learning. Third, students are reading, writing, making inferences, thinking critically, using music, using dance, and being creative, to interact and connect with the content's main ideas and reinforce long-term learning.

How to Use the Activity

This activity can be offered as one of several choices for students to display their learning. Students may work in groups, pairs, or individually on this project. They should understand the meaning of the term *theme*," the message being communicated by the artist.

Students should preview examples of music and dance clips as models for discussion. This activity may need several days or class periods to preview, plan, create, practice, and share. Depending on the background of the students and their experiences with the artistic world, background knowledge may need to be developed on types of music, the history of dance, and interpretation of the humanities. It might be helpful to bring in a speaker, a music teacher, or a dance teacher.

After students have chosen their examples, both music and lyrics should be previewed before the content is shared with the class. It is important that students have planning conferences and perhaps have a teacher sign off on the idea before they begin sharing a song or dance with the entire class.

Evaluation

The assessment of this activity can involve several steps. The stages to grade are planning and choosing the music or dance, cooperating with partners, conferencing e with the content teacher, writing and explanation of the activity in two paragraphs, and performing or sharing the song or dance with the other students in the class.

Variation(s)

Students who are more adept with technology could use music and pictures to create a thematic collage or a digital story based on the theme or main ideas of the topic.

39. USING MUSIC AND DANCE TO LEARN

Directions: Use your creativity to choose one of the 2 forms listed to communicate a message from the reading.

Title of Text: _____

Choice 1: Find a **song with lyrics** that communicates the theme, message, feeling, or content of the text that you have read. Write or type the lyrics, find a recording of the song to present to the class, and write an explanation of the meaning of the song and an explanation of the connection of the song to the content of the reading. (Of course, all lyrics must contain appropriate language, and the teacher will preview the material if there is a question.) Time limit for the piece of music is 2–3 minutes.

Preview Plan for Project 1

1. Name of reading and/or book _____

2. Title of song _____

3. Title of recording artist _____

4. Write or type the lyrics and time the song or part of the song being used. Time: _____

_____

_____

_____

5. Write a paragraph explaining the meaning of the song and how the music and words communicate that meaning. State the theme, message, or feeling. _____

_____

_____

_____

_____

6. Write a paragraph explaining the connection of the theme, message, or feeling to the reading material. _____

_____

_____

_____

(1 of 2)

Choice 2: Create a 2–3 minute **choreographed dance** to a music selection to communicate a theme, message, or feeling from the text that you have read. Find a recording of the music to use in class and write an explanation of the meaning of the song and how the dance connects to the music and the text. (Of course, all lyrics and movements must be appropriate, and the teacher will preview if there is a question.) Performance time limit is 2–3 minutes.

Preview Plan for Project 2

1. Name of reading and/or book _____

2. Title of song _____

3. Title of recording artist _____

4. Write or type the lyrics (if the music contains lyrics) and time the song or the part of the song being used. Time: _____

_____

_____

_____

5. Write a paragraph explaining the meaning of the song and how the music, words, and movements communicate that meaning. State the theme, message, or feeling.

_____

_____

_____

_____

_____

_____

_____

6. Write a paragraph explaining the connection of the theme, message, or feeling to the reading material. _____

_____

_____

_____

_____

_____

_____

(2 of 2)

From *Reading and Writing to Learn: Strategies across the Curriculum* by Katherine Kuta. Westport, CT: Teacher Ideas Press. Copyright © 2008.

Activity 40

Information Poster

Purpose of the Activity

The purpose this activity is to improve students' understanding of content. By interacting with the text through searching for a direct quotation for connection, expressing their feelings in words, stating the key main concepts, writing a summary, and drawing visuals for memory cues, students' understanding of material increases. Students will learn to be accurate, creative, and succinct in their writing, because all the information must fit on a one-page promotional poster for the topic.

How to Use the Activity

Have students display ownership of their learning by having them teach one another about the content using the handout for activity 40, which asks each individual or pair to display very specific information. Assign a section of a chapter, reading, or book to students to read, take notes, and create the one-page poster. Have some students share the information while others take notes on the presentations. Display the finished posters. Use the handout as a rough draft.

Evaluation

Evaluate this activity for content as well as expressing the information in a clear, concise manner. Since a visual is being used for teaching, the creativity and presentation of the page are also factors to consider.

Variation(s)

In addition to sharing what they learn, students could walk around the room and write down in their notebooks one idea that they want to remember from each poster.

Another variation is to ask students to create brochures on the poster topics to present to the class.

40. PROMOTIONAL AD POSTER

Name: _____

Directions: Create a, single-side, visually attractive, promotional page about your assigned reading. Follow the plan shown in the boxes for displaying your information. Your project must be **accurate and creative and contain all the listed information.**

2. List 3 adjectives that describe your feelings about the book. Write a sentence explaining each adjective, using an example from the book.

Two pieces of clipart or pictures taken from a magazine or Web site to draw attention to the page

1. State a direct quotation from the book that you believe connects to you or the message of the book. Use quotation marks and cite the page number. Explain your choice in 2 sentences.

3. Title (underline it):

Author:

Publisher and year:

Type of book (genre):

Two pieces of clipart or pictures taken from a magazine or Web site to draw attention to the page (symbols, people, or events):

5. Write a 3- to 5-sentence summary

4. State the theme, message, or major concept of the book in 1 sentence.

Part 3

Writing to Learn

Activity 41

Writing to Learn: Two-Column Notetaking

Purpose of the Activity

The purpose of two-column notetaking is to provide an organized system for students to actively read nonfiction materials such as textbooks, which require slow and interactive reading. Since many students need practice reading their textbooks for a purpose, the "RECALL" column in handout 41B gives students the chance to create questions from the headings, if present; to watch for boldface vocabulary; and to be aware that each paragraph has at least one main idea. The "NOTE" column is larger and allows space for the students to record their answers to the questions on the left, explain definitions, list important details, or add visual memory cues. Students also need to learn how to take notes in an efficient manner that can be used for reviewing and studying at a later date. This form of notetaking helps students organize information.

How to Use the Activity

As best practices suggest, the notetaking procedure should be modeled more than once before asking students to move to guided practice and eventually to independence. At the beginning of the informational reading selection or textbook chapter, point out the structural features of the content reading, such as illustrations, diagrams, headings, boldfaced concepts, paragraphs, sections, or other distinctive features. Students need to learn to read content as a specialist in that field would read it. Students have a tendency to read everything in the same manner, but a math textbook is structured very differently than a social studies textbook or a science textbook.

After the notetaking process, have students highlight, mark asterisks next to, or draw a box around the key ideas in pairs. By working in pairs, students learn from one another and can review their notes again. Review with students how to use their notes to study for a test. Have them cover the right side of the handout with their books or folders and ask themselves the questions in that column. If they cannot remember or understand the material, then they need to re-read, study, or label the information that needs more studying. "Study buddies" or pairing can be useful for practicing oral fluency and reviewing of the material.

Evaluation

Depending on the purpose, this notetaking activity could be graded as a homework activity or as a participation grade for the classroom. Students could be given points for working on their own as well as points for sharing and adding additional notes (in a different color) from discussions in class. The evaluation is asking the students to process and comment on the learning strategy. If the students recognize an improvement on their test scores or grades, then they will continue using the strategy and have ownership of their own learning.

Variation(s)

This activity can also be used with fiction. The RECALL column can be used to record visual scenes from a story, and the NOTE column can be where the students enter their explanations of the scenes For English Language Learners or special education students, all the notes could become visual memory cues for the questions or words in the left column.

41A. TWO-COLUMN SYSTEM OF NOTETAKING

DATE
LABEL CLASS/TEXT NOTES
PAGES OF TEXT

RECALL	NOTE COLUMN
What do you do? (6)	**STEP 1-BEFORE THE LECTURE OR READING** 1. Get out paper or notebook for particular class. 2. Use only one side as directed. 3. Draw 2½ line from the left side of paper. 4. Take notes on the right side only. 5. Put key words, phrases, and questions on the left side. 6. Review notes BEFORE the next class.
What do you do during the notetaking? (8)	**STEP 2-DURING THE LECTURE OR READING** 1. Record notes in your own words. 2. Don't outline unless teacher directed. 3. Listen for main ideas to write down. 4. Skip lines between major ideas. 5. Use few abbreviations. 6. Write clearly so it makes sense later for studying. 7. Leave space for day dreaming so you can fill it in later. 8. Do not copy notes over because it wastes time.
What do you do after the notetaking? (8)	**STEP 3-AFTER THE LECTURE OR READING** 1. Read through your notes. 2. Make scribbles readable. 3. Fill in blanks and check out ? and blank spaces. 4. Make main ideas stand out by using boxes, circles, underlining, or highlighting. 5. Fill in the recall column with key ideas or questions on right side. 6. **For studying, cover up the right side.** 7. **Say out loud the facts and ideas needed to answer the question on left.** 8. **Check your answers by uncovering the right side.**
SUMMARY	**TRY TO WRITE A SHORT SUMMARY (3–5 SENTENCES) OF WHAT YOU LEARNED FROM YOUR NOTETAKING**

From *Reading and Writing to Learn: Strategies across the Curriculum* by Katherine Kuta. Westport, CT: Teacher Ideas Press. Copyright © 2008.

41B. NOTETAKING TO LEARN AND REMEMBER

Name: _____

Topic and Pages: _____ **Date:** _____

Recall Column	Note Column
Choices: Question from a heading Keywords = main idea/picture (Hint! Each paragraph has at least one main idea or boldfaced word.)	Use bullets for supporting details (Each idea should not have more than 8 words. Do not write in complete sentences.)

What do I know now that I didn't know before taking these notes?

_____

_____

_____

From *Reading and Writing to Learn: Strategies across the Curriculum* by Katherine Kuta. Westport, CT: Teacher Ideas Press. Copyright © 2008.

Activity 42

Writing to Learn: Foldable

Purpose of the Activity

This activity is a hands-on approach to notetaking for visual and kinesthetic learners. Students make their own foldables to use as directed for content learning, and they can later use them to study for a test. Students are directed to take specific notes in both words and picture form. The pictures become the "memory cues" for the concepts.

How to Use the Activity

First students need a sheet of blank paper. Have them use larger paper than the standard size to allow for more creativity and visibility for sharing with the entire class. Different colors can be used for various units to keep students organized. First have students hold a blank piece of paper vertically and fold it so that the two ends meet in the middle of the paper. The result is two flaps with an opening in the center, similar to two swinging doors that meet in the middle. The center line on handout 42A represents the meeting of the two flaps. Next have them fold the sheet of paper in half twice so that there are eight creases in the paper. The they should place scissors in the opening between the two flaps and cut on the creases so that there are four boxes on each front panel. They should then use handout 42A as a guide to label the eight boxes on each front panel. For the inside of the foldable, have them open the two flaps with the eight boxes; there should be sixteen boxes. At the top of each box in the foldable they should copy the words shown on handout 42B. (See page 170 for how to do this activity.)

Use handout 42C for practice with a content lesson. As a lesson is taught or text is read, direct students to stop and make notes in both words and pictures. If the activity is being completed in class, after students make their entries, use a **think-pair-share activity** for students share ideas with one another. The repetition of the concepts increases comprehension.

Evaluation

The foldable activity can be evaluated as a class activity, homework, or notetaking study guide activity. Students should be judged on accuracy and completeness.

Variation(s)

The words on the flaps of the foldable may be the headings in a chapter, the concepts from a unit, the elements of a story, the elements of a movie, major vocabulary words, or titles of books shared during booktalks. The back of the entire foldable can also be used for students to assess their own learning. An example would be to ask them to write down three ideas that they want to study again before the test, a summary of the lesson, strategies used for increased understanding, or even how the foldable helped their learning.

42A. WRITING TO LEARN: NOTETAKING FOLDABLE (OUTSIDE)

Foldable to Process Information

Connection to (background information)	A feeling about the topic
1 vocabulary word	One question that I want to ask
1–2 concepts from my reading	1–2 concepts from the class discussion
A picture to help remember a concept	Something that I want to share with others

42B. NOTETAKING FOLDABLE (INSIDE)

Name: _____

In Words	In Pictures	In Words	In Pictures

In Words	In Pictures	In Words	In Pictures

In Words	In Pictures	In Words	In Pictures

In Words	In Pictures	In Words	In Pictures

Step 1: Place a blank sheet of paper horizontally or vertically in front of you.

Step 2: Fold in fourths so that the 2 end panels meet in the center but do not overlap each other.

Step 3: Fold in half again by bringing the top of the paper to the bottom of the paper.

Step 4: Fold the paper again by bringing the left flap to the right side so that it now appears like a small book.

Step 5: Fold the foldable again one more time.

Step 6: Unfold the paper so that it looks like step 2 but it has 4 folds on the end panels and 8 folds in the center when it is opened. Use scissors to make 3 cuts on the folds of the end panels. The result is 4 separate boxes on each panel.

Step 7: At the top of each box, label it on the panel as directed.

Step 8: Open the panels and label each of the 8 boxes which were created by the folds in the center of the foldable.

42C. WRITING TO LEARN: NOTETAKING FOLDABLE

Name: _____

Foldable to Process Content Lesson Information

Connection to (background information)	A feeling about the content lesson topic
1 vocabulary word	**One question that I want to ask**
1–2 concepts from my reading	**1–2 concepts from the class discussion**
A picture to help remember a concept	**Something that I want to share with others**

From *Reading and Writing to Learn: Strategies across the Curriculum* by Katherine Kuta. Westport, CT: Teacher Ideas Press. Copyright © 2008.

Activity 43

Writing to Learn: Processing Information Boxes

Purpose of the Activity

The purpose of this processing guide is to increase critical thinking and understanding. By writing a "skinny" (literal) question and a "fat" (inference) question, students get the opportunity to practice writing questions and become familiar with the question stems that are used on state and ACT reading tests. Students also learn to connect with the text by responding to an open-ended sentence. Finally, students practice creating visual memory cues to increase comprehension of important concepts.

How to Use the Activity

At the end of a period, a lesson, or a day, ask students to process one, two, or all of the boxes on the handout. Before the activity is used with the entire class, students should understand the difference between the two types of questions that are being requested. Model both types of questions for the group. Make sure that students are aware that "skinny" question stems consist of "who, what, where, and when" and that the answers to "skinny" questions are found directly in the text. "Fat," or inference, questions have stems that begin with "Why is this important?" How does this connect to me?" The ACT reading test uses the stems, " The author suggests . . ." and "The author implies . . .". By repeatedly being asked to write and answer their own questions, students will begin to automatically use this deeper meaning skill as they read on their own.

Students are asked to write a reflection sentence in the third box on the handout. By thinking critically about their own learning, students begin to think and write about it and accept ownership.

Students are asked to draw a visual memory cue in the fourth box for a concept that they feel is important or that is being focused on in class. By drawing, students are connecting to the core of the concept in a way that makes sense to them. A discussion can take place in class or a review can take place the next day or class period.

Evaluation

One way to assess understanding and have all students engaged is to use a cooperative activity called "Numbered Heads." As students complete the processing sheet, assign them numbers from one to four. Ask the number 1s to stand and take turns reading their "skinny" questions aloud. Depending on time and purpose, the questions could be discussed or the class could engage in a "thumbs up/thumbs down" activity. If the question is a "skinny" question, then students should vote "up," and if the question is not a "skinny" question, the vote should be "down." The teacher should not vote but should count to three so that all vote at the same time. Then ask the number 2s to stand and share their "fat" questions, and the number 3s to share their reflection statements. Finally, have the number 4s stand and share their visual memory pictures. Collect the activity sheets and grade them on participation.

Variation(s)

One variation for this activity is to cut apart the boxes containing the "skinny" and "fat" questions the students have written and ask students to put them in two shoeboxes, one for "skinny" questions and one for "fat" questions. Then students could choose one question from each box and answer each question in a roundtable discussion.

43. WRITING TO LEARN: PROCESSING INFORMATION BOXES

Name: _____

Topic: _____ Pages: _____

| Skinny (Literal) Question |
| Literal: Who, What, Where, When; answer is in the text |

| **Fat Question** |
| **Inference: Why, How, Explain; The text suggests . . .** |

| Reflection Statement (1–3 Sentences).Choose one: |
| I learned . . ., I want to look at . . . I want to try . . . I want to know more about . . . |

| Visual Memory Cue for the Concept of _____ |
| (Using words and pictures to remember an important idea) |

Activity 44

Writing: Daily Reflections

Purpose of the Activity

The purpose of this "writing to learn" activity is to give students the opportunity to reflect on their learning, write their ideas on a graphic organizer, and demonstrate ownership of their learning. If they are absent during this activity and are unable to fill in the handout, students must be accountable and contact a "buddy" to obtain the assignment, offer a reason for their absence, and attach the box explaining the absence to the makeup work.

How to Use the Activity

Enough copies of the handout should be made to be used for several weeks. Students can cut apart the boxes to attach them to a class assignment or homework if desired. Another possibility is to have the students fill in the boxes on a daily basis but collect the worksheet only at the end of the week. Students need time to process, so allow a few minutes for them to think, reflect, look back at notes, and write about a concept and a vocabulary word. For kinesthetic learners, ask students to "walk and talk" to share one idea with five different classmates and have each listener initial the handouts.

Evaluation

This activity should be assessed as any other class activity would be assessed. Determine a point value for completing the task, writing in complete sentences, and processing the information. If students are involved in a research project, have them use the activity worksheet with cited material that supports their thesis.

Variation(s)

The processing handouts serve as feedback from the students for teachers to see to which concepts, vocabulary, and other information the students connected with. If there are misconceptions, then more extended practice, reinforcement, or reteaching may be necessary.

Remember that some students may be more comfortable sharing in picture form, so a memory cue could be added on the back of the sheet.

44. WRITING TO LEARN: DAILY REFLECTIONS

Processing: What Did I Learn This Week?

Week: _____ **Date:** _____ **Name:** _____ **Class/period:** _____ What did I learn today? (complete sentence) Define 1 new concept or vocabulary word:	**Week:** _____ **Date:** _____ **Name:** _____ **Class/period:** _____ What did I learn today? (complete sentence) Define 1 new concept vocabulary word:
Week: _____ **Date:** _____ **Name:** _____ **Class/period:** _____ What did I learn today? (complete sentence) Define 1 new concept or vocabulary word:	**Week:** _____ **Date:** _____ **Name:** _____ **Class/period:** _____ What did I learn today? (complete sentence) Define 1 new concept vocabulary word:
Week: _____ **Date:** _____ **Name:** _____ **Class/period:** _____ What did I learn today? (complete sentence) Define 1 new concept or vocabulary word:	**Week:** _____ **Date:** _____ **Name:** _____ **Class/period:** _____ What did I learn today? (complete sentence) Define 1 new concept vocabulary word:

Activity 45

Writing Poetry: Metonymy

Purpose of the Activity

This activity offers students practice using the form "metonymy" to write poems about abstract concepts in content disciplines. (Metonymy is a figure of speech in which one word or phrase that is "concrete," physical or tangible, is substituted for another word that may be "abstract," conceptual, or intangible.) Comprehension is increased because students are connecting their prior knowledge of concrete information with a new abstract concept. Students are engaged in writing for the purpose of gaining ownership of their own learning as well as sharing with their classmates. Because increasing interactions with content increases memory and learning, this activity offers students another interaction with textual concepts.

How to Use the Activity

Use the activity during or after a reading and writing experience. After the students have finished reading a section of text or at the end of a chapter, assign students to create three poems using the major concepts of the reading. Model a concept poem in class. Direct students to work in pairs on one poem so that they gain confidence and familiarity with the form. Students will use poetry to explain concepts covered in their content area classes, such as freedom, individualism, photosynthesis, polynomials, congruent triangles, imperialism, or nutrition. The concepts chosen should be major ideas that students need to know and remember.

Have students display and share their poems.

Evaluation

Assess this activity as a class or homework writing assignment. Some features to consider are following directions, meeting a deadline, completion of the activity, creative, concrete examples, and sharing work with the class.

Variation(s)

One addition to this activity to appeal to visual learners is to ask students to accompany their poems with color and pictures. By adding these features, the brain is more responsive to connecting the old with the new information. Ask auditory learners to include background music in their reading of their poems. Ask kinesthetic learners to add movement or dance to the poetry.

45. WRITING POETRY

A Metonymy Poem
Defining an Abstract Word with Concrete Examples

Directions: Using the concept words from the present unit of study, choose 3 topics and create poems to help define the term in concrete lines of poetry.

- Remember that the concrete examples must enable the reader to see, to hear, to smell, to taste, and/or to feel the concept.

- Remember that abstract words are intangible and nonrepresentational and more difficult to understand, or may have multiple meanings.

Example:

Summer

Sleeping late in the mornings

Licking ice cream cones

"Hanging out" with friends

Reading a book for fun

Staying up late and wishing the day will not end

Freedom

Being able to vote

Being able to make one's own decisions

Being able to say "no"

Winning the American Revolution

Living in the United States

_____ (abstract concept)

_____

_____

_____

_____

_____ (abstract concept)

_____

_____

_____

_____ (abstract concept)

_____

_____

_____

_____

From *Reading and Writing to Learn: Strategies across the Curriculum* by Katherine Kuta. Westport, CT: Teacher Ideas Press. Copyright © 2008.

Activity 46

Writing: The Power of Three

Purpose of the Activity

There are several purposes for the "power of three" exercise. Students must think critically about their own knowledge and assess which three concepts they still need to learn. They will interact with their choices by defining the concepts in fewer than ten words and thinking of a memory cue for each of the words. Since fewer than five words are transferred to long-term memory weekly, students need to interact with concepts repeatedly and often to ensure learning. Many students need seven to ten interactions with words before those words are "owned."

How to Use the Activity

This activity should be used as a process writing exercise. Model this activity first, because students may not be used to explaining a concept in a few words. Eventually students may work in pairs for guided practice to gain comfort and ensure success. The independent stage adds individual ownership of ideas that need to be identified for future review.

Evaluation

Award class participation points for completion of this activity.

Variation(s)

Ask students to cut out the boxes in the handout and place them on index cards to keep and study for future assessments. This activity could be used as an ongoing learning activity by having students file, string together, staple, or organize the boxes in some way for future reference.

Another variation of the "power of three" is oral sharing. Ask for three student volunteers. By sharing their content ideas, students will repeat them rather than just hearing the teacher do so. This practice can be done several times within a class period or a school day. By stopping, processing the information, and sharing it, students' learning is increased.

46. WRITING TO LEARN: THE POWER OF THREE

Name: _____

Directions: After writing the major concepts from the day, lesson, or unit, choose the 3 most important concepts that will help increase understanding and memory. Then write the main idea in 10 words or less in boxes below. Also, think of a memory cue visual to help picture the information.

Record the vocabulary, terms, concepts from notes and reading material here and circle the three that you want to focus on remembering:

Text: _____

Pages: _____

List of Key Concepts:

1. _____

2. _____

3. _____

Contents Material: _____

Concept: _____

In words: _____ _____ _____

_____ _____ _____

_____ _____ _____

Visual Memory Cue:

(1 of 2)

Contents Material: _____

Concept: _____

In words: _____ _____ _____

_____ _____ _____

_____ _____ _____ _____

Visual Memory Cue:

Contents Material: _____

Concept: _____

In words: _____ _____ _____

_____ _____ _____

_____ _____ _____ _____

Visual Memory Cue:

Activity 47

Writing: Facts vs. Opinions

Purpose of the Activity

The purpose of this activity is to improve students' visual understanding of the difference between two major concepts, facts, and opinions when reading and writing and to provide an opportunity for guided practice.

How to Use the Activity

Model the concept of "fact vs. opinion" to the whole group. Use the first section of either a fiction or nonfiction text for the lesson. To determine facts in nonfiction, have students look for statistics and numbers, commonly accepted knowledge, or undisputed, provable information. In fiction, the reader suspends his or her beliefs and assumes the world that the author has created to be true, so the author's descriptive details become "facts."

Tell students that opinions in nonfiction consist of the author's thesis or focus and quotes from other authorities on the topic. In fiction, the opinions are either stated directly by the characters in dialogue, or through an omniscient author.

A variety of texts can be used to for guided practice in this activity. Use news articles for students to analyze for facts. Use feature articles or human interest stories for students to find both facts and opinions. After this process has been modeled, students may examine their content textbooks and other types of readings to become more proficient at this skill with guided practice. Pairs of students may be assigned a reading and work together to find and record examples of facts and opinions. Students may share and evaluate the examples they have found in a whole class discussion.

Evaluation

Evaluate this activity as a class activity, homework assignment, or cooperative exercise. Assign points to students for participating in the process, not necessarily on the number of correct responses.

Variation(s)

Have students use this important skill in for a research project. Ask them to share their research notes with one another for guided practice throughout the process of learning how to do research.

47. WRITING TO LEARN: FACTS VS. OPINIONS

Directions: Carefully read and observe the facts and the opinions in the assigned reading. Write facts in the squares, and opinions in the circles.

FACT: can be proved, is undisputed, has concrete evidence
OPINION: a belief, a value, can be argued

Title: _____

Author: _____

What did you learn from this activity? _____

_____

_____

Activity 48

Writing a Memo

Purpose of the Activity

The purpose of this writing activity is for students to practice a specific form of authentic writing, the memo, for the purpose of sending an interoffice communication. By writing to a teacher with the purpose of setting goals, students learn the difference between the memo and other forms of writing, such as e-mail, a letter, an essay, or notetaking.

How to Use the Activity

Because students learn best from modeling, collect sample memos from school correspondence, online, or from writing instruction books. Ask student to make observations and comments about how this form of writing differs from other forms of writing with which they are familiar. By looking at samples, making their own observations, and discussing their findings, students are involved in their own learning, as opposed to the teacher explaining and directing the lesson. Display a list of their observations on the board or overhead for students to record.

Use the activity 48 handout as a template for students. Students should type up a perfect final copy. If students change classes and have multiple teachers, they may be asked to write to a particular teacher and set goals for the class that they think need special attention.

Evaluation

This activity could be used as a formal writing example in a student's portfolio. The previewing, rough draft, and final draft could all be graded separately.

Variation(s)

If the focus of the lesson is on forms of writing, a variety could be given to the students to peruse and make observations. Students need to understand the differences among an e-mail, a memo, a business letter, a friendly letter, a brochure, a postcard, a thank you note, text messaging, and other forms of communication. Students also need to understand which forms of writing are formal and which are informal.

48. WRITING A MEMO FOR COMMUNICATION

A memo is used for interoffice communication, and you are going to write an authentic memo to one of your teachers at school, explaining the goals that you are going to work on this semester in that particular class. Use the template below to write your rough draft. Remember to use blue or black ink, and proofread it when you're done.

Date: _____

Name of Teacher: _____

Name of Class: _____

RE: Goal Setting to Improve Success

Goals: _____

_____

_____

How I plan to achieve my goals: _____

_____

_____

_____

Interschool Memo

Date: _____

To: _____

From: _____

Re: _____

_____

_____

_____

_____

_____

_____

_____

_____

_____

_____

From *Reading and Writing to Learn: Strategies across the Curriculum* by Katherine Kuta. Westport, CT: Teacher Ideas Press. Copyright © 2008.

Activity 49

Writing an E-mail for a Specific Audience

Purpose of the Activity

There are several reasons for having students practice this type of writing. First, because e-mails are a part of students' daily lives, they need to learn how to use them efficiently for various audiences. Students need to learn the importance of constantly being aware of whom the receiver is and to practice writing an e-mail that is brief, concise, and understandable. E-mails are direct and to the point. Students like to write the same way they talk, so they need to understand that informal abbreviations that are acceptable to use with friends are not appropriate when addressing a teacher or in the business world.

How to Use the Activity

Practice this activity on paper. Ask the class: "Why are e-mails used in the world?" and "How are e-mails used in the world?" Students will know that e-mails provide immediate feedback in an increasingly busy world, provide "free" communication, and make use of computers, which are widely available. Model several business e-mails that you have received. In order to help them understand that both purpose and audience are important when writing an e-mail, give students the handout and ask them to first write an e-mail to a peer asking for assignments that they missed while absent from school. Then ask them to practice writing the same e-mail request to a teacher. Ask students to help each other revise the e-mail (using a different color pen) to improve word choice and content. The important feature of this activity is the discussion of students in pairs about the communication and the differences between the two e-mails. The last question on the handout asks the students to process their own learning, which requires the students to think and write a reflection.

Evaluation

This activity could be counted as both a class grade and an individual writing grade. Some features to consider are the clarity of the content, the conciseness of the message, proper word choice, and fulfillment of the assignment.

Variation(s)

If the students have access to e-mail accounts, they can use this form of communication to contact other students for homework assignments they have missed. Require students to find a homework "buddy" who would be required to take handouts for the absent partner and e-mail that student describing what happened in class and reminding him or her about deadlines. By taking responsibility for makeup work, students are more involved in teamwork and ownership of learning.

49. WRITING AN E-MAIL FOR COMMUNICATION

E-mail is used for written communication in business and for pleasure. Remember that the message should be concise, accurate, and clearly stated. The type of language that is used depends largely on the audience for the message.

Directions: Write 2 e-mails, communicating to (1) a classmate and (2) the teacher that you are ill. Request missed assignments for the day that you were absent from school.

E-mail to a Teacher

E-mail to a Classmate

How do the messages differ? _____

_____

_____

What did you learn from this activity about communication? _____

_____

_____

Activity 50

Writing a Want Ad

Purpose of the Activity

There are two purposes for this assignment. First, students need to become more aware of purpose and form in writing. The want ad is used specifically in newspapers and on the Internet to advertise for a specific person, object, service, or employment. Because space is money, this form of writing requires careful word choice, summarization skills, and the ability to communicate a great deal in a small amount of space. Second, students will practice critical thinking and formulate ideas on the different qualities and skills that are necessary for a a good student, a good teacher, and a good parent.

How to Use the Activity

Use this activity in the classroom or as a homework assignment. If newspapers are available either in the classroom or in the library, have students preview and read actual want ads. Another option is to cut out ads before class and pass them around for students to read. Ask students to choose one and then write out the information in the ad in regular prose, to show that they understand the abbreviations used in ads.

Students need to realize that whatever they write down first is not necessarily their best writing or best communicates their ideas. Have them use the back of the handouts to brainstorm the qualities and skills for the type of job or person they are seeking in the want ad and then write a rough draft. Have students pair and share so that partners can assist each other in choosing words, condensing the information, and offering positive ideas about the content. Have students make revisions using different colors of ink and then write the ads in the boxes on the handouts. Ask students to count the words and put the number in a circle next to each box. Finally, discuss how this specific type of writing differs from other forms. Ask students to share their writing aloud.

Evaluation

Since this activity involves a writing process, each step of the process may be counted as a participation grade, or the final product can be graded at the end. The activity should be assessed in terms of following directions, completion of the writing, and whether the content makes sense.

Variation(s)

For the varied subject areas, the type of want ad could be changed. For example, in social studies class, the ad could focus on a leader, soldier, survivor, president, diplomat, or other historic role. For science, the ad could focus on an inventor, scientist, researcher, or other kinds of people in the field. For business, there are many possibilities, such as a person in marketing, advertising, finance, accounting, or other careers that students may be familiar with. For math, the ad could seek computer programmers, mathematicians, or math teachers. In English, students could write ads seeking characters in stories as "missing persons."

With the explosion of online dating services, students could even be asked to pretend that they are writing an ad looking for a boyfriend or girlfriend to be posted with one of these companies.

50A. WRITING TO LEARN: WRITING A WANT AD

Directions: Preview want classifieds and other ads in the newspaper to observe how words and phrases are shortened (abbreviated and condensed). This is done because customers pay by the word and the amount of space used in an ad. Then write 2–3 want ads. Use the back of this paper to write rough drafts. Do not use more than 30 words in each want ad. Count the words used in each ad and write that number next to the ad in a circle.

Title of Newspaper: _____

Date: _____

Type of Want Ad: _____

Observations: _____

_____

_____

Want Ad for a Good Student

Want Ad for a Good Teacher

Want Ad for a Good Parent

50B. WRITING TO LEARN: WRITING A WANT AD FOR A SPECIFIC JOB

Name: _____

Want Ad for a Person Needed for a Specific Job in a Content Area Field

Directions: Focusing on the content area being studied and the special jobs and careers in a particular field, research the requirements for a particular job and then write a want ad for it. Write the job description in regular prose and then convert it into a want ad. Each letter costs five cents, and you can spend no more than $5.00, or in other words, no more than 100 letters or spaces.

Handwritten Description: _____

_____

_____

_____

_____

_____

_____

Want Ad for the Specific Job

Activity 51

Writing: Say It with Pictures

Purpose of the Activity

This activity involves content material, reading skills, writing skills, and speaking skills. Students are asked to focus on key ideas, themes, or concept words and critically think about a visual to represent the main point, then find a photo, a clipart picture, or other artwork to display the meaning or feeling. By asking students to interact with the content and synthesize the concepts, comprehension is increased and there is ownership of learning. In addition, the students must use their writing skills to explain their choices as well as the significance of each visual. Finally, students are asked to "show and tell" their work so that class members can learn from one another.

How to Use the Activity

Use this post-reading or -writing activity at the end of a lesson, unit, or book. For fiction, the focus can be on the events of the plot or the themes, universal messages, or symbols of the story. For nonfiction in a content class or unit in a book, the focus can be conceptual vocabulary, important facts, historical events, an era, or important people.If three concepts are being required per person, pair, or team, then the number of items for review must match the number of students. For example, if there are ten teams of two students each, then twenty items must be prepared for distribution. There are two ways to distribute the items. One is to ask students to brainstorm the important information, make a list, pass it out in class, and self-select the items by signing their names next to them on the list. Another possibility is to prepare a list of items and assign them to individuals, pairs, or teams. If possible, allow time for students to browse clipart and art on computers. After handout 51 has been completed, ask students to give mini-presentations in front of the class and share the visuals and explanations with the class. Ask class members to record the items and memory cues in their notes to help them prepare for a future assessment.

Evaluation

This activity can be assessed at several levels. Grade students on following directions, participation, completion of the assignment, expository writing, and speaking skills during the presentation. Class members can also be given a grade for note taking.

Variation(s)

To involve students kinesthetically, ask them to stand up and, while holding their pictures, arrange themselves according to (1) a sequence of events for a unit in history; (2) the steps in a scientific process; (3) the events of a story plot; or (4) the terms for each chapter in a unit, in which case there may be multiple groups.

51. WRITING TO LEARN: SAY IT WITH PICTURES

Chapter, Unit, or Story: _____

Directions: You will be assigned 3 IMPORTANT concepts, words, terms, people, themes, formulas, or main ideas from the content being studied. Find 3 photos, pieces pf clipart, or other artwork that best represent the idea. Put the images in the boxes provided. Then write a short paragraph explaining the relationship of the visual to the assigned words. Be prepared to show and share on _____.

1. Concept: _____

_____

Explanation: _____

_____

_____

_____

2. Concept: _____

_____

```
┌────────────────────────────────────────────────────────┐
│                                                          │
│                                                          │
│                                                          │
│                                                          │
│                                                          │
│                                                          │
│                                                          │
│                                                          │
└────────────────────────────────────────────────────────┘
```

Explanation: _____

_____

_____

_____

3. Concept: _____

_____

```
┌────────────────────────────────────────────────────────┐
│                                                          │
│                                                          │
│                                                          │
│                                                          │
│                                                          │
│                                                          │
│                                                          │
│                                                          │
│                                                          │
└────────────────────────────────────────────────────────┘
```

Explanation: _____

_____

_____

_____

(2 of 2)

Activity 52

Writing a Friendly Letter to a Pen Pal

Purpose of the Activity

There are several purposes for this writing activity. The first is to have students learn the form of communication, the friendly letter. The second is to have students write to other students about themselves, synthesizing their own learning and increasing their comprehension.

How to Use the Activity

Find another class in your school or at another school, or possibly another type of students such as English Language Learners, with whom to exchange letters. Students will be more motivated to write to other students who will answer their letters rather than just writing as an exercise. Consider doing an exchange of letters only once each quarter; it may take several drafts to get an acceptable final letter to send .

Students learn from models, so display several examples for students to view. A mini-lesson should be given on acceptable letter forms, especially the "modified block and block" style. Have students prewrite and list ideas that they could include on the back of the activity handout, then use the front to create their rough drafts.

Remind students that, to maintain the reader's interest, most letters are only one page long. Through peer editing, students can advise each other about content and revisions. Ask students to type or neatly write their final drafts. Personal information such as phone numbers, addresses, and other specific data should be left out of the letter. All letters should be turned in and passed on to the pen pal group by the teacher. If the specific pen pals' names are unknown for the first exchange, then tell the students to just write, "Dear Pen Pal,". Make sure that students have proofread and fixed all mistakes as well as signed the final copy in ink.

In terms of format, the first paragraph should include information about the letter writer. The second paragraph should focus on connections to the readings in class. The third paragraph should include questions for the pen pals to respond to when they write back.

Evaluation

It might be helpful to ask students to make two copies of the final drafts of their letters, one copy to be graded and stored in the students' portfolios, and one to be passed on to the pen pal group. Staple together all the documents created during the writing process and store them in the students' writing portfolios.

Variation(s)

The focus for each round of correspondence can be different. However, by writing about the content material that they are reading and studying, the students are increasing their own comprehension. One paragraph in the letters could focus on specific concepts being studied, and another could focus on a particular book or reading.

52. WRITING A FRIENDLY LETTER TO A PEN PAL

Directions: Write a friendly, 3-paragraph letter to a student whom you may never meet in person. A pen pal can be in your school or in another country. Use formal English and correct all mistakes. The student will write back to you based on the information in this letter. This letter will be in "modified block style". Use this form to write a rough draft. The final draft should be typed or handwritten legibly.

Modified Block Format:

[Write out date] _____

Dear Pen Pal,
[In paragraph 1, write a 5–7 sentence introduction about yourself. Include a brief background, your hobbies, your interests, and your classes.]

_____

_____

_____

_____

_____

[In paragraph 2, write 5 to 7 sentences about the stories, books, and other reading that you have done this year so far. Explain which selections you liked and why.]

_____

_____

_____

_____

_____

[In paragraph 3, ask 3 to 5 questions that you would like to have answered. Ask general questions about interests, books, hobbies, and classes.]

_____

_____

_____

_____

_____

Sincerely,
[Sign your name in ink]
[Type your name]

From *Reading and Writing to Learn: Strategies across the Curriculum* by Katherine Kuta. Westport, CT: Teacher Ideas Press. Copyright © 2008.

Activity 53

Letter to Next Year's Students: How to Be Successful in Class!

Purpose of the Activity

The purpose of this activity is to offer students an authentic writing experience, writing to other students. When writing this letter, students will look back at their work and reflect on their performance in the class. Students are asked to share specific study skills, learning techniques, and words of wisdom based on their experiences in a particular content class. Incoming students will have the opportunity to read the letters at the beginning of a course and gain insights into that class.

How to Use the Activity

Near the end of a grading period, ask students to reflect on their learning in the class. Have them make a list of skills and strategies that helped them improve their learning. Have students use the handout to draft a letter to the next students coming to the class, sharing their "words of wisdom" in the first paragraph. Ask students to write a second paragraph about what they would change if they had the opportunity to begin the year over again.

Evaluation

Assess this writing as a typical formal writing assignment in terms of format, the writing process, content, grammar, and mechanics. Tell students to strive for excellence because the letters will be shared with future students. The next group of students will read this after a year of growth as readers and writers.

Variation(s)

Ask eighth graders or seniors in high school to reflect on their time in school and ask what they would have done differently in grammar school or high school that they want to share with incoming students.

53. LETTER TO NEXT YEAR'S CLASS

Name: _____ (block style) _____

How to Pass my _____**Class!**

[Write out date:] _____

Dear Students _____:

After completing this course, _____, with my teacher,

_____, I would like to make a few suggestions to you to add to your

success in the class. [First paragraph should be at least 10 sentences long and include at

least 5 tips.] The first tip is _____

_____.The second tip is

_____

_____. The third tip is

_____

_____

_____. The fourth tip is _____

_____

_____. The fifth tip is _____

_____.

    If I had the opportunity to begin the year over again, I would make several changes. The

first would be _____

_____

_____. The second would be _____

_____

_____.

The third would be _____

_____.

The words of wisdom that I would share with future students in this grade would be

_____

_____

_____.

 Sincerely,

[Sign your name]

[Type your name]

From *Reading and Writing to Learn: Strategies across the Curriculum* by Katherine Kuta. Westport, CT: Teacher Ideas Press. Copyright © 2008.

Activity 54

Steps in the Writing Process

Purpose of the Activity

The purpose of this checklist is to empower students through their writing and learning. Students need to understand that "writing" is a complicated process that involves many steps and constant revision. In this activity they are required to keep track of each step in the formal writing process. Another purpose of this activity is for students to realize that the writing process is used for communication and that "writing to learn" increases understanding and ownership of learning.

How to Use the Activity

To show students that not all writing is done at one sitting, this process checklist helps add organization and structure to the process. Students can use this checklist for narrative, expository, and persuasive essays. This checklist can also be used for a single- or multi-level paragraph paper. Each step of the checklist should be taught and evaluated throughout the process. At the end of the writing process, this sheet may be attached to the top of the final paper.

Evaluation

To teach accountability, assign a point value to each step of the writing process. At the end of the process, assign a grade to the final worksheet.

Variation(s)

Steps of the checklist may be modified as necessary. One variation is to add areas of specialization that need to be evaluated on the rough and/final drafts. An example is the terms for the state writing rubric, such as the focus sentence, which could be highlighted in yellow or italicized in the first and last paragraphs. Another area of the rubric is support, and it might be helpful to ask students to highlight the specific support or use the computer to underline or boldface the specific support in each paragraph. A third part of the rubric is organization. By adding transitions to their papers, the text structure becomes more evident and there is more cohesion and coherence in the paper. A possibility for pointing out transitions is to ask students to highlight at least three transitions in each paragraph or use the computer to boldface the words and phrases that provide connections.

The focus in writing could also be on various items of grammar or usage, depending on the current lesson. Some ideas to emphasize are the parts of speech, subjects and predicates, topic sentences, clincher sentences, word choice, sentence variety, or other areas covered by the state/ACT writing rubric.

54. FORMAL WRITING CHECKLIST

The Writing Process

Use this reference sheet for your planned essay writing. Check off each step as you complete it.

Directions: Date and check off each step of the process, then attach this sheet to your final paper.

_____ 1.   **Prewriting Choices**
              Clustering/mapping
              Free writing
              Brainstorming
              Using a graphic organizer

_____ 2.   **Focus = Thesis = One sentence = Main idea for paper**

_____ 3.   **Plan for Paper = Text Pattern**
              Topic and details for each paragraph

_____ 4.   **First Draft = Rough draft with errors**

_____ 5.   **Peer Editing = Reading draft aloud to peers for them to listen for a purpose**
              Student writes "One positive comment"
              Student writes "One helpful comment" to improve/content, focus, support, or transitions

_____ 6.   **Revision = Making changes to improve paper**

_____ 7.   **Proofreading = Correcting errors and making sure all makes sense**

_____ 8.   **Final Draft = Error free paper**

_____ 9.   **Self-evaluation = Write 1 or 2 sentences explaining what you learned in this assignment**

_____ 10.   **Highlight special features as directed or use**

              Italics _____, Underlining _____

              Boldface _____ (if using the computer)

From _Reading and Writing to Learn: Strategies across the Curriculum_ by Katherine Kuta. Westport, CT: Teacher Ideas Press. Copyright © 2008.

Activity 55

Formal Writing Plan for Argumentation (Persuasive Writing)

Purpose of the Activity

The purpose of this activity is to provide a graphic organizer to aid students in planning a formal, persuasive essay. Because the ACT writing test now expects students to produce an organized, argumentative essay in 30 minutes, students need to practice the format for a well-organized paper in both timed and untimed settings. Students will become familiar with the features of a formal essay and understand that an introduction includes an attention getter, focus, and basic preview of the major arguments of the essay. The body of the paper includes transitions, major support, specific support, explanation of the support, and clincher /concluding sentences. The rebuttal paragraph involves thinking and writing about the opposite side's views and refuting them. The conclusion sums up the paper, restates the focus, and ends with words to be remembered by and make an impact on the reader. Make sure that students realize that before they write they must think and plan out their ideas in a specific format (which varies with the purpose of the writing).

How to Use the Activity

This activity should be included as part of the writing process for students to plan and make a rough draft. Depending on the skills of the writers, each part of the paper could be taught and checked individually, in steps. By means of mini-lessons throughout the writing process, model how to write an introduction, refine a focus/thesis sentence, develop support for the focus (including reasons and specific, concrete support), and sum up with a conclusion. Eventually students will automatically use the basic format for both timed writing and independent writing.

Evaluation

The handout should be used during the peer editing stage of writing, in which groups of four students create a "Writer's Circle" and each person takes a turn reading aloud. As the other members listen, they should write two comments for each reader on slips of paper. The first comment is something "positive" that they liked about the content of the paper. Examples are "a clear and well stated thesis" or "the rebuttal included some ideas that were in my mind while you were reading." The second comment should be a helpful (constructive) criticism. In other words, students should consider the variety of transitions, the supporting arguments, the concrete, specific support, the thesis, and the conclusion. You may also direct them to listen for other specifics. Remind students that grammar is not the focus of their comments;

rather, they should comment on the continuity and the articulation of the purpose of the paper. Count both activities as a grade in the writing process before the final draft grade.

Variation(s)

The activity handout may be changed and revised for expository or narrative essays. Tell students that a rebuttal paragraph is not included in those forms of writing. Also point out various transitional words needed to make connections and provide text structure.

55A. WRITING PLAN—FORMAL WRITING: PERSUASION/ARGUMENTATION

Introduction

Attention Getter: _____

Transitional Sentence: _____

_____

Focus Declarative Sentence: _____

_____

_____

(State 3 arguments in a sentence if not in above focus) _____

_____

_____

_____

Reason 1: Body Paragraph 1

Transition _____, **Topic sentence:** _____

_____

_____

_____

Transition _____, **Support 1 and explanation:** _____

_____

_____

_____

Transition _____, **Support 2 and explanation:** _____

_____

_____

_____

Transition _____, **Support 3 and explanation:** _____

_____

_____

_____

Clincher/summary sentence: _____

_____

_____

(1 of 3)

Reason 2: Body Paragraph 2

Transition _____, **Topic sentence:** _____

_____

_____

Transition _____, **Support 1 and explanation:** _____

_____

_____

Transition _____, **Support 2 and explanation:** _____

_____

_____

Transition _____, **Support 3 and explanation:** _____

_____

_____

Clincher/summary sentence: _____

_____

_____

Reason 3: Body Paragraph 3

Transition _____, **Topic sentence:** _____

_____

_____

Transition _____, **Support 1 and explanation:** _____

_____

_____

Transition _____, **Support 2 and explanation:** _____

_____

_____

Transition _____, **Support 3 and explanation:** _____

_____

_____

Clincher/summary sentence: _____

_____

_____

From *Reading and Writing to Learn: Strategies across the Curriculum* by Katherine Kuta. Westport, CT: Teacher Ideas Press. Copyright © 2008.

Rebuttal (the other side)

Transition _____ **, Topic sentence:** _____

_____

_____

_____

Transition _____ **, Support 1 and explanation:** _____

_____

_____

_____

Transition _____ **, Support 2 and explanation:** _____

_____

_____

_____

Transition _____ **, Support 3 and explanation:** _____

_____

_____

_____

Clincher/summary sentence: _____

_____

_____

Conclusion

Transition _____ **, Repeat focus differently:** _____

_____

_____

_____

Summarize main points: _____

_____

_____

_____

Clincher sentence: _____

_____

_____

55B. WRITER'S CIRCLE: PEER EDITING

Student Critic: _____
Type of Paper: _____
Title of Paper: _____ **Date:** _____

1. Write one positive comment on the paper.
_____
_____
_____

2. Write one helpful comment to improve the paper.
_____
_____
_____

Name of Reader: _____

Student Critic: _____
Type of Paper: _____
Title of Paper: _____ **Date:** _____

1. Write one positive comment on the paper.
_____
_____
_____

2. Write one helpful comment to improve the paper.
_____
_____
_____

Name of Reader: _____

Student Critic: _____
Type of Paper: _____
Title of Paper: _____ **Date:** _____

1. Write one positive comment on the paper.
_____
_____
_____

2. Write one helpful comment to improve the paper.
_____
_____
_____

Name of Reader: _____

Student Critic: _____
Type of Paper: _____
Title of Paper: _____ **Date:** _____

1. Write one positive comment on the paper.
_____
_____
_____

2. Write one helpful comment to improve the paper.
_____
_____
_____

Name of Reader: _____

Activity 56

Timed Writing Checklist

Purpose of the Activity

The purpose of this activity is to help students organize their writing to prepare for a timed writing portion of a test. If students repeatedly practice using their time efficiently, they will be able to follow the activity's format automatically during timed tests, such as in state writing tests or ACT writing exams.

How to Use the Activity

After reproducing the student handout, preview the information on it in class by having the students actively highlight the material while reading it. All the types of essays, such as *narrative, expository,* and *persuasive,* should be defined and reviewed. At the beginning of a class period or during a 30–35-minute time slot, hand out a writing prompt and tell students that they will be timed while they are using the format on the handout. Read the directions aloud together. Give students five minutes to plan the writing, which should include an attention getter, focus, and major support. Say "stop" when the five minutes are up. Next time the students for 20 to 25 minutes while they write the draft. (Adjust the time for the particular test you are preparing for. For example, the ACT writing test is 30 minutes long.) After the allotted time, say "stop." For the last 5 minutes, students should finish, proofread, and read over their writing. Then say "stop" again.

Then have the students assess their progress using the activity 56 handout. They should identify their weaknesses. They may use highlighters to color code various parts of the essay. For example, students could highlight the focus with yellow, supports in the body paragraphs with pink, and transitions in the paragraphs with blue. If the writing was a persuasive/argumentative essay, the rebuttal could be coded green. If any of these areas are missing, students need to set a goal of including them in the next practice. If students did not finish the writing, then they need to think about timing. Remind students that although the writing is being evaluated as a "draft," a complete draft is needed.

On the back of the writing, students should write down three goals for improvement.

Evaluation

Because timed writings can be stressful for students, the practice timed writing in class could be counted as a class participation activity. Additional points can be given for the self-evaluation part and goal setting.

Variation(s)

Students could take turns reading their timed writings in a "Writer's Circle" and be asked to complete the checklist for one or two of their peers. After several practice timed writings, ask students to choose their best writing for sharing.

56. FORMULA FOR WRITING FOR A TIMED ESSAY WRITING TEST

Name: _____

Read the directions and the prompt very slowly and decide on the type of writing being asked for, such as **narrative, expository, or persuasive**.

Plan the writing: (first 5 minutes)

Attention getter: _____

_____

Focus = thesis sentence: _____

_____

Preview of major support for body paragraphs: _____

_____

_____

_____

Write the draft of the paper clearly: (20–25 minutes depending on length of test)
Remember to include:

- Introductory paragraph
- Support paragraphs with specific, concrete examples
- Rebuttal paragraph if the essay is persuasive
- Conclusion

Proofread the writing: (last 5 minutes)

Check and correct the following:

- Spelling
- Run-ons
- Sentence fragments
- Indentation of for each paragraph
- Clearly stated focus in the introduction and conclusion
- Title that is fewer than 8 words long
- References to newspaper, magazines, and books underlined
- References to articles, poems, and short stories quoted
- Continuous point of view throughout the writing

Tips:

- Watch the clock constantly and judge your time.
- Write clearly so that a stranger can understand what has been written.
- Finish the test.
- Make sure you are doing what is asked in the prompt.
- Be aware of word choice, and use formal language and variety.

From *Reading and Writing to Learn: Strategies across the Curriculum* by Katherine Kuta. Westport, CT: Teacher Ideas Press. Copyright © 2008.

Activity 57

Writing to Learn: Writing for a Younger Audience

Purpose of the Activity

This exercise gives students a chance to review content concepts by asking them to rewrite the main points of a reading in simpler language for a younger student. Research states that comprehension increases to as much as 90 percent when students simplify concepts or teach them to someone else.

First the students write out the major concepts from the text. Then they think about and restate the ideas for a younger person to understand, which forces them to use nontechnical language that is less difficult than that in the textbook. Finally, students create a memory cue to help them teach and remember the information. By sharing with one another, students repeat the major concepts, and their learning will increase.

How to Use the Activity

Tell students that this activity is a writing exercise to help them remember major concepts from a lesson. In the real world, writers are constantly aware of their target audience. Students need practice keeping in mind the purpose of their writing and their audience. Too often, students only write formally for the teacher and very informally for their friends.

Model this exercise to the class the first time it is introduced. Ask students about taking care of their siblings or about babysitting and discuss how these experiences require using different language for younger children.. Then offer other examples of audiences: the principal, an employer, a parent, an absent friend, a store clerk, or others. Discuss these questions: "Why should the type of language change for a particular audience?" "How does a writer change language to communicate more clearly with a particular audience?" Word choice, sentence variety, paraphrasing, and revision are all necessary skills for writers to develop. Mini-lessons about any of these aspects are appropriate.

After students write out the concepts in clear sentences on the handout, have them use the back of the sheet to practice restating the concepts for a younger audience. Students may work in pairs to achieve the best clearly restated ideas, making revisions in a different color ink. Once the concepts have been restated, then the students can think of pictures, shortened versions, graphics, or organizers to set the ideas in their long-term memory as well.

Ask students to share one of their concept rewrites and the matching memory cue with the group. Direct students to record one to three ideas that they still need to learn and remember from the sharing. Place this sheet in the students' binders for future reference.

Evaluation

Students may be evaluated on the individual steps of the activity or on the activity as a whole.

Variation(s)

There are two suggested variations for this activity. The first is to change the audience each time students are asked to write, so that there is variety and increased motivation. The second is to ask students to teach more in the classroom. By randomly choosing a concept to teach or review with the class in some way for one or two minutes, students increase their comprehension.

57. WRITING TO LEARN: WRITING FOR A YOUNGER AUDIENCE

Directions: To increase understanding of the major concepts, pretend that you have been asked to explain the major ideas to someone who is 5 years younger than you.

- First, write out 3 to 5 concepts as clearly as possible.
- Then rewrite them for the other person.
- Share your responses with your partner.
- Choose a memory cue for each idea.

Topic of Text: _____

_____

Major Concepts:

1. _____
2. _____
3. _____

Younger Audience Rewrite:

1. _____
2. _____
3. _____

Memory Cues:

Concept 1	Concept 2	Concept 3

From *Reading and Writing to Learn: Strategies across the Curriculum* by Katherine Kuta. Westport, CT: Teacher Ideas Press. Copyright © 2008.

Activity 58

Writing: Paraphrasing

Purpose of the Activity

The purpose of this activity is to have students practice rewriting text in their own words in order to increase comprehension. Often students take notes directly from the textbook exactly as it is written, without trying to paraphrase or summarize. When doing research, students need to be able to use this skill to take notes to support their focus. In this activity, students will practice with short pieces of text to improve their notetaking skills as well as come to understand the term *paraphrasing*.

How to Use the Activity

Because some students may not be familiar with this writing skill, teach a mini-lesson on paraphrasing, explaining the purpose of the skill and modeling with content material from a textbook, article, or newspaper. As guided practice, have students use the activity worksheet with one assigned piece of text and work in pairs. Have students display their rewordings for the class to determine which passage rewrite best communicates the same ideas in the same number of words. Have students pass around the paraphrases in groups (without names) and rank the order of the paraphrases from 1 to 10, with 1 being the best.

For a second piece of text, have students draw passages on slips of paper from a box or hat and work in pairs to paraphrase the chosen text. Preparation would involve duplicating and cutting up important text passages for students to discuss. Ask students to share their paraphrases aloud while classmates take notes on the key concepts and evaluate the rewritten text.

Evaluation

Use the activity as either a class grade or a homework grade.

Variation(s)

If students are involved in a research project, have them use the activity worksheet with cited material that supports their thesis.

58. WRITING TO LEARN: PARAPHRASING

Directions: Write the assigned text on the lines below. Then restate the same ideas in the **same length** and with the **same meaning**, in your own words. Share your writing with your partner and choose the "best wording" to use in revising so that the meaning is closest to the original.

Paraphrase the directions here: _____

_____

_____

_____

Sample text 1

_____

_____

_____

Your paraphrase

_____

_____

_____

Paraphrase revised with partner: _____

_____

_____

_____

Sample Text 2

_____

_____

_____

Your paraphrase

_____

_____

_____

Paraphrase revised with partner: _____

_____

_____

_____

Activity 59

Summary Writing

Purpose of the Activity

This writing exercise is designed to give students explicit practice in learning how to read a paragraph, think about the text, and recap its meaning in a short summary. The goal is to help students realize that each paragraph has at least one main idea and support for it. When asked to write a summary paragraph, they will practice using a beginning, middle, and end. It should also become evident that it is more difficult to write a shorter summary, because it requires a more concise focus on the important points, and the lesser details need to be condensed or eliminated. This activity can be used with textbooks, research material, or any type of nonfiction. Summary writing for fiction is equally important, but it requires summarization of the whole rather than each paragraph. Finally, students are asked to think about the strategy and write about their own learning.

How to Use the Activity

Depending on the skill level of the students, this strategy may have to be modeled several times for the whole group. If the text being read has more than five paragraphs, then additional paper or content notebooks will be needed. By checking at least five summary notes for the first five paragraphs, the teacher can judge whether the students understand the task and the material.

If introducing summary writing for the first time, explain to students what it is and why they are learning about it. In a class discussion, students can brainstorm the kinds of careers and jobs that would require this important writing skill. Also note that in doing research, the reader must be able to summarize the text for support for the focus and must give credit to the author of the resource for his or her ideas.

For this activity, prepare a mini-lesson about the difference between main ideas and details. Sometimes the main idea is unstated, and all the details add up to the key idea of the text. Textbooks are structured differently in different disciplines. Students need to understand the format and structure of the text that they are reading. Very often publishers use boldface headings, italicized keywords, indented paragraphs, space between paragraphs, bulleted lists of chapter ideas, sidebars, and other format features, which students sometimes overlook. Since students have a tendency to write too much or too little, tell them they must use all of (and only) the space allotted on the handout. Remind them that summary writing may require multiple revisions to reach a desired result.

To model summary writing on the board, computer, or overhead, start with the topic or section heading and ask the 5 Ws as an aid in reading for a purpose: Who or what is it about? What is being said? When? Where? Why? plus How?

Define new terms and provide examples using them. If a process is described, the sequence must include the steps in order. In social studies, there are names, places, dates, and abstract ideas to note. In

215

science, there are technical terms, processes, and math involved. Students need to read in each content area as a specialist in that field would read the material. Each content area has its own demands.

After the modeling, students should work in pairs on the same text so that they can discuss the ideas for guided practice. Assign small chunks of reading to be done within a reasonable time, so that students will have greater success with the process. The handwritten summaries may be revised and typed. Also, the activity sheet may be used to record notes to review for a quiz or test. A class discussion based on the summaries would allow students to hear the information again and evaluate their own work.

Evaluation

The summary notes can be graded as a class or homework activity. To involve students even more in the assessment process, ask them to use a highlighter while the summary notes are being discussed to mark the key words, phrases, and ideas that should be present in their notes. Students may correct or add ideas to their own work with a different color pen. Points may be given for the number of correct ideas that were included in the summaries.

Variation(s)

If the students are reading for research notes, have them use larger index cards to record the summary. Another suggestion is to alter the handout so that the focus is on one source of research per page. Make sure to include an area for the bibliographic source information.

59. WRITING: SUMMARIZING

Name: _____

Directions: As a post-reading or -writing strategy to increase your understanding, complete the chart, summarize each section of the reading material. Condensing the main ideas and major details will help you remember what you read. **Remember that the shorter the summary, the more concise you need to be.**

If there are 5 paragraphs in a section of the reading, then there should be at least 5 main ideas supporting the main topic.

Section Title: (look for boldface words if applicable) _____

Paragraph 1: Key idea and important details: _____

_____

_____

Paragraph 2: Key idea and important details: _____

_____

_____

Paragraph 3: Key idea and important details: _____

_____

_____

Paragraph 4: Key idea and important details: _____

_____

_____

Paragraph 5: Key idea and important details: _____

_____

_____

Summary of Section: Using the key words and details from the lines above, write a summary of the section in complete sentences. Boldface or highlight the key words and phrases.

_____

_____

_____

_____

What do you know now that you did not know before you completed this strategy?

_____

_____

From *Reading and Writing to Learn: Strategies across the Curriculum* by Katherine Kuta. Westport, CT: Teacher Ideas Press. Copyright © 2008.

Activity 60

Letter of Self-Evaluation to the Teacher

Purpose of the Activity

There are several purposes for this writing activity. The first is to have students learn to use the business letter format for communication. Second, students evaluate their own learning by using all their materials as supportive details for the body of the first paragraph. Students also assess their skill growth in paragraph 2, and in paragraph 3 they focus on their weaknesses or lack of understandings and areas for future improvement. These letters from students offer excellent feedback to teachers.

How to Use the Activity

This writing activity can be used in any content area at the end of a grading period. If the letter is assigned before the final examination, teachers will get information on areas of strength and weakness that may need to be reviewed. This letter itself could be used as a final exam. Give students time in class to organize their materials for easy reference. Use another class period to write the rough draft. If possible, schedule students in a writing lab to type the professional letter, signed and accompanied by all parts of the process for the teacher to evaluate. For accountability, ask students to highlight their examples in each paragraph so that they are more aware of the specific details they are using for support.

Evaluation

Grade this writing assignment following the school, state, or ACT writing rubric with which students are familiar. If the letter is being used as final exam, grade the entire thing for content.

Variation(s)

Teachers or students could generate a list of the units, concepts, important terms, etc., that were pertinent to the course, as an aid in reviewing the material.

60. WRITING A LETTER OF SELF-EVALUATION

Name: _____

Directions: This writing activity involves writing a business letter to your teacher in block style, evaluating your learning this semester in this class. You may use your textbook, handouts, former assignments, notes, and your folder to gather ideas for specific details for your paragraphs. Letters should be perfect and 1 page in length, so grammar and format are very important. Remember to proofread. You may use this sheet for you rough draft.

[Write out date:] _____

Dear Mr. Mrs. Ms. _____:

[First paragraph should be at least 10 sentences long, include at least 5 major key ideas, and explain using details from different units of study.] During this semester in your class of _____, I have learned several important concepts that I will remember in the future. The first is _____

_____.

The second concept is

_____

_____

_____

The third concept is

_____

_____

_____

The fourth concept is

_____

_____

_____

The fifth concept is

_____

_____

_____

Finally, the most interesting lesson was the unit on _____

_____, because _____.

From *Reading and Writing to Learn: Strategies across the Curriculum* by Katherine Kuta. Westport, CT: Teacher Ideas Press. Copyright © 2008.

[For paragraph 2, write 7-10 sentences about learning skills that you acquired and improved on, such as notetaking, studying, etc. List at least 3 skills and examples.] In addition to the content material, I learned other life skills, study skills, and reading/writing skills that I will use in other courses in school. These include

_____,

_____, and _____

_____.

I improved on the first skill of _____ by

_____

_____

I improved on the second skill of _____ by

_____

_____

I improved on the third skill of _____ by

_____

_____

The area in which I think I most improved is _____, because

_____

_____

_____.

[In the third paragraph (5 sentences), write about what you still need to work on, learn, or improve on in the content area.] There are 3 areas that I still need to work on and improve on in the future:

_____

_____

_____

_____

_____

_____

Sincerely,
[Sign your name]
[Type your name]

(2 of 2)

References

Allen, Janet. 2000. *Yellow Brick Roads: Shared and Guided Paths to Independent Reading 4–12.* Portland, ME: Stenhouse.

Beers, Kylene. 2003. *When Kids Can't Read What Teachers Can Do: A Guide for Teachers 6–12.* Portsmouth, NH: Heinemann.

Blachowicz, Camille, and Donna Ogle. 2001. *Reading Comprehension.* New York: The Guilford Press.

Burke, Jim, and Ron Klemp. 2002. *Reader's Handbook: A Student Guide for Reading and Learning.* Boston: Houghton Mifflin.

Burmark, Lynn. 2002. *Visual Literacy: Learn to See, See to Learn.* Alexandria, VA: ASCD.

Daniels, Harvey. 1994. *Literature Circles: Voice and Choice in the Student-Centered Classroom.* Portland, ME: Stenhouse.

Daniels, Harvey, et al. 2007. *Content-Area Writing.* Portsmouth, NH: Heinemann.

Fogarty, Robin. 1997. *Brain Compatible Classrooms.* Arlington Heights, IL: Skylight Training and Publishing.

Gallagher, Kelly. 2004. *Deeper Reading, Comprehending Challenging Texts, 4–12.* Portland: Stenhouse.

Glasgow, Neal A., and Cathy D. Hicks. 2003. *What Successful Teachers Do: 91 Research-Based Classroom Strategies for New and Veteran Teachers.* Thousand Oaks, CA: Corwin Press.

Green, Marguerite. 1997/1998. "Rapid Retrieval of Information: Reading Aloud with a Purpose." *Journal of Adolescent and Adult Literacy* 41, no. 4 (December/January).

Harvey, Stephanie, and Anne Goudvis. 2000. *Strategies That Work: Teaching Comprehension To Enhance Understanding.* York: Stenhouse.

Irvin, Judith L., et al. 2003. *Reading and the High School Student: Strategies to Enhance Literacy.* New York: Allyn and Bacon.

Jennings, W., and J. Caulfield, J. 1997. "Moving Your School to Brain Compatibility." In *The Networker.* Alexandria: ASCD.

Jensen, Erik. 2005. *Teaching with the Brain in Mind.* 2d ed. Alexendria: ASCD.

Johnson, D. W. and R. T. Johnson. 1989. *Cooperation and Competition: Theory Research.* Edina, MN: Interaction Book Company.

Keene, Ellin Oliver, and Susan Limmermann. 1997. *Mosaic of Thought.* Portsmouth, NH: Heinemann.

Kuta, Katherine Wiesolek. 1997. *What a Novel Idea! Projects and Activities for Young Adult Literarture: Projects and Activities for Young Adult Literature.* Westport, CT: Teacher Ideas Press.

Langan, John. 1992. *Reading and Study Skills.* 5th ed. New York: McGraw.

Marzano, Robert. 2004. *Building Background Knowledge for Academic Achievement: Research on What Works in Schools.* Alexandria: ACSD.

Marzano, Robert J., Debra J.Pickering, and Jane E. Pollock. 2001. *Classroom Instruction That Works: Research Based Strategies for Increasing Student Achievement.* Alexandria: ASCD.

Moore, David W., Patricia M. Cunningham, et al. 1998. *Developing Readers and Writers in the Content Areas K–12.* New York: Longman.

Pauk, Walter. 1997. *How to Study in College.* Boston: Houghton Mifflin.

Scarborough, Harriet Arzu. 2001. *Writing Across the Curriculum in Secondary Classrooms: Teaching from a Diverse Perspective.* Upper Saddle River, NJ: Merrill Prentice Hall.

Sousa, David. 2006. *How the Brain Learns.* 3d ed. Thousand Oaks, CA: Corwin Press.

Strong, William. 2006. *Write for Insight: Empowering Content Area Learning, Grades 6–12.* New York: Pearson.

Tate, Marcia L. 2003. *Worksheets Don't Grow Dendrites.* Thousand Oaks, CA: Corwin Press.

Tierney, R. J., and T. Shanahan. 1991. "Research on Reading-Writing Relationships: Interactions, Transactions, and Outcomes." In *Handbook of Reading Research,* Volume 2, edited by M. Barr Pearson and P. B. Mosenthal. New York: Longman.

Tovani, Chris. 2004. *Do I Really Have to Teach Reading? Content Comprehension, Grades 6–12.* Portland: Stenhouse.

Ziegler, Linda L., and Jerry L. Johns. 2005. *Using Mental Images: Visualization to Strengthen Comprehension.* Dubuque, IA: Kendall/Hunt Publishing, 2005.

About the Author

Katherine Kuta has lived her whole life in the Chicagoland area in Illinois and has more than thirty years' experience teaching kindergarten through college level. However, the majority of her career has been spent working with high school students in English, reading, and science. She considers the adolescent learner the most challenging but also the most rewarding for her as a teacher.

She currently teaches English, works with students as a reading specialist, and works with teachers as a literacy coach at Maine East High School, District 207, in Park Ridge, Illinois. She is also an adjunct faculty member in the reading department at National Louis University in Wheeling, Illinois, and offers workshops in "reading and writing across the curriculum." In her spare time she is a freelance writer. She is active in several professional organizations, including the International Reading Association, and often presents at conferences and other schools.

By working and associating with many professional educators, authors, and a variety of students, Katherine feels that she is constantly learning. She wants to share with others her successful strategies and engaging lessons that improve student learning in the classroom. She believes that reading improves writing and writing improves reading, so students must be involved in both areas.

In addition to reading, writing, and teaching, Katherine likes to travel, play tennis, and spend time with her family. She has a supportive husband and one 15-year-old daughter, whom she enjoys watching grow and mature as a young adult on a daily basis. Katherine finds it fun to discuss books with one's own child. The one thing that her daughter always reminds her mom to remember when creating activities and projects to share with her teachers is that the create activities and assignments should be for *students to do, and not for adults to do for them.* The activities and strategies in this book were created with this suggestion in mind.

Because all lifelong learners must be readers and writers, Katherine wants teachers to use this book to engage students in two important processes, reading to learn and writing and learn, in all subject areas for the rest of their lives.